MESSIAH

RICK ROTONDI

CENACLE.TV

Copyright © 2019 by Rick Rotondi

All rights reserved.

No part of this book may be reproduced in any form or by any electronic or mechanical means, including information storage and retrieval systems, without written permission from the author, except for the use of brief quotations in a book review.

Scripture texts used in this work are predominantly author paraphrases or common or traditional renderings.

Scripture texts marked NABRE are taken from the New American Bible, revised edition © 2010, 1991, 1986, 1970 Confraternity of Christian Doctrine, Washington, D.C. and are used by permission of the copyright owner. All Rights Reserved. No part of the New American Bible may be reproduced in any form without permission in writing from the copyright owner.

Cenacle
Charlotte, NC
SeeMessiah.com

These are written that you may believe that Jesus is
the Messiah, the Son of God, and that by
believing you may have life in his name.

— John 20:31

CONTENTS

Prologue	1
1. Exodus	3
2. David	29
3. Exile	50
4. Trial	71
5. Ascension	92
6. Pentecost	114
7. Paul	138
8. Triumph	159
Notes	181
About the Author	193
About Messiah	195

PROLOGUE

Are you the king of the Jews?

Pilate's question to the prisoner before him rang through the crowd. All held their breath in anticipation.

The king of the Jews. *The Messiah.*

For almost a thousand years, the Jewish people had been waiting for him. For long centuries, they had suffered, enduring the splitting of their kingdom, the scattering of their people, the destruction of the Temple and the loss of the Ark.

They had been conquered and made captive by pagan nations. They had drunk the bitter cup of slavery and defeat.

One promise sustained them: that a son of David would come who would restore the kingdom in its fullness.

This anointed king, this Messiah, would gather back the lost tribes. He would make Israel, not a prisoner to pagans, but a light unto them.

He would make firm the Temple sacrifice forever. And he would be powerful, placing all enemies under his feet.

Now Pilate had voiced the question burning in their hearts. Here was a man who spoke with authority, who was more powerful than storms and disease and demons. Here was a man with a zeal for the Temple, a man who, in calling the Twelve, had begun, at least symbolically, to reassemble the twelve tribes.

Yet here he was also before Pilate, meek as a lamb, not as a conqueror but as a prisoner. Could this captive really be king?

Messiah is an exploration of the kingship of Jesus such as you have never experienced before. It is an investigation of the messianic prophecies and expectations of ancient Israel. It is the answer to Pilate's question and that of the crowd around him, the question posed to each one of us. And it is an unforgettable encounter with Jesus as savior, shepherd, and king.

1

EXODUS

A PEOPLE SET APART

The trial of Jesus is the most famous in history. When it took place nearly two thousand years ago, it galvanized all Jerusalem.

Jesus was brought before the Jewish court, the Sanhedrin. He was accused of blasphemy, of claiming divinity by referring to himself with the words I AM,[1] and he was found guilty.

The Jews were an occupied people, powerless to execute the death sentence. The Roman governor Pontius Pilate would have to render judgement. The Jewish leaders brought Jesus, bound, before him.

The trial of Jesus fascinates us still. The charges boil down to a central question that echoes through the ages—as crucial and hotly debated today as it was then.

It is a question recorded in all four Gospels,[2] asked by Pilate as Jesus stood captive: *Are you the king of the Jews?* And it is a question posed to Jesus by the high priest Caiaphas the night before: *Are you the Messiah?*[3]

There is no more important question we can ask. To answer it well, we must unpack that mysterious title, *Messiah*.

Its literal meaning is "Anointed One," the equivalent of the Greek word *Christos*, or Christ.

Yet *Messiah* suggests more: a priest who will build God's Temple; a prophet who will speak for the Lord; a long-promised king who will liberate God's people, conquer their enemies, and place them under his feet.

The word *Messiah* has so many layers of meaning that the only way to unravel them is to journey back through the centuries when these layers were acquired. Only then can we fully answer the question posed to Jesus at his trial: *Are you the Messiah?*

The first step of our journey takes us to when Israel was established as a nation. It is a moment when—as at the trial of Jesus and so many times in their history—the Jews were oppressed by a foreign power.

And it is a moment when the Lord would rescue them in dramatic fashion, claim them for himself, and lead them as their king.

To be a Jew is to be a descendant of Abraham by way of Isaac and then Jacob. Jacob, later known as Israel, fathered twelve sons. Their descendants became the famous twelve tribes of Israel.

While the Jews, or Israelites, became a people through God's covenant with Abraham, it took them hundreds of years to become a nation.

That occurred with the Exodus from Egypt, over 1,200 years[4] before Christ.

The Exodus is the defining event in Jewish history. It is the means by which the Lord brought the Israelites to their homeland and revealed himself as their king.

The Promise of a Nation

Chapter 12 of Genesis records how God called Abraham and promised to make of him a great nation. It is a promise God affirms repeatedly. Yet generations pass, and the promise remains unfulfilled. Abraham's descendants multiply, yes. But famine drives them from their land. They flee to Egypt and remain there.

The first to arrive is Jacob's favorite son, Joseph. He arrives as a slave. God had told Joseph through a dream that one day he would rule over his brothers. When Joseph shares the dream, his brothers seethe with jealousy. *Are you really going to make yourself king over us?* they ask. They plan to kill him; then, at the suggestion of Judah, they betray and sell him instead. The price? Twenty pieces of silver.[5]

It is an inauspicious beginning. Yet God is with Joseph, and despite obstacles and setbacks, he rises to a position at Pharaoh's right hand.

Joseph orders the establishment of massive grain reserves in Egypt's cities. God has warned through dreams given to Pharaoh, and interpreted by Joseph, of a coming seven-year famine. Joseph wisely prepares.

When the famine strikes, Egypt is fed. Joseph's brothers are not so fortunate. They come to Egypt desperate for food. They seek to buy grain from Joseph, who during the famine must personally approve all exports. Joseph recognizes his brothers immediately, but for a time, he conceals his own identity. When he reveals it, his brothers are terrified. The brother they betrayed is alive, full of authority, with the power to save them or cast them out. They deserve the latter; yet Joseph reassures them. *You meant to harm me,* he will explain, *but God meant it for good.*[6]

It is the very act of his brothers' betrayal that puts in motion God's plan to bring Joseph to Egypt, empower him, and save many from death.

Joseph resettles his brothers and their father, Jacob, in Egypt. Jacob is overcome at his reunion with Joseph and the working of God's Providence. Later he will give Joseph a double inheritance. He will adopt Joseph's sons Ephraim and Manasseh.[7] Both will be numbered among the twelve tribal patriarchs of Israel, forming what is known as the "house of Joseph"—one of the two great genealogical lines among the Israelites. The other is the house of Judah, concerning which Jacob makes a prophecy: *The scepter will not depart from Judah . . . until Shiloh comes.*[8] It's an obscure prophecy, but it suggests that Judah will rule among the Israelites until the mysterious event or person referred to as Shiloh arrives. Later commentators will see in Shiloh a reference to the Messiah.

The Israelites flourish in Egypt. Pharaoh, grateful to Joseph for his service, gives Joseph's family the pick of the land. He receives Jacob's blessing in return. As time passes, however, and the Israelites multiply, the Egyptians' hospitality crumbles.

When a new Pharaoh comes to power, one that *knew nothing of Joseph,*[9] the Israelites are enslaved. They are forced to make bricks for Egypt's massive building projects. Their workload is raised, and raised again. Pharaoh turns the screws on their chains tighter and tighter still.

Scripture recounts how the Israelites groaned under their bondage, crying out to God. They yearned for freedom but didn't have the strength to rebel.

Egypt was the dominant power of the age, the Rome of its era. The Pharaohs were the most powerful men on earth. Egypt's neighbors were vassal states. Whenever their leaders addressed Pharaoh, they referred to themselves in the most obsequious terms: *the ground on which you walk, your throne, the footstool of your feet.*[10] Pharaohs reinforced and encouraged such cravenness through their royal décor. It was common to depict prisoners and foreigners on their floors and footstools so that the Pharaohs might literally trample their images under their feet.

Let My People Go

For years the Israelites endure their bondage. Then Pharaoh makes a fatal error. He turns the screws on the Israelites' manacles one twist too tight.

As another king, Herod, will do over a thousand years later, Pharaoh orders a massacre of innocents. Threatened by the growing number of Israelites, he orders all their newborn boys cast into the Nile River.

That leads to one boy being rescued and raised in Pharaoh's palace. The boy, Moses, grows to be a prince of Egypt and, after his experience at the burning bush, a prophet of the Lord.

Moses will end by becoming, like Joseph, a great savior of God's people—the greatest perhaps except for the Messiah. As with Joseph before him, Moses' leadership is initially resisted. Moses is a member of the Egyptian royal family, and he loves the Israelites. He burns with anger at their servitude and even recklessly kills an Egyptian taskmaster. Later he intervenes in a dispute among the Israelites. His attempt at mediation is rejected. *Who has appointed you ruler and judge over us?*[11] one asks.

After this, and fearing the consequences of his killing of the Egyptian taskmaster, Moses flees Egypt for Midian. There Moses marries, fathers two sons, and works as a shepherd. Moses is content with this life and has no ambition to return to Egypt. But the Lord has a plan for Moses.

He reveals it when Moses brings his sheep to the mountain of the Lord, Sinai, and discovers the burning bush.

At the burning bush, Moses experiences what's known as a *theophany*—a self-revelation or disclosure by God. The Lord tells Moses to remove his sandals, since he is standing on holy ground. Then God reveals his Divine Name, one so mysterious that to this day we cannot be certain how it is pronounced. We know it only by the four letter *tetragrammaton*, *YHWH* in Latin, usually rendered *Yahweh* in English.

The name *Yahweh* would become so sacred to the Jewish people that to write it or speak it aloud was blasphemy. The Jews developed the custom of substituting a title such as *Adonai* ("the Lord") for *Yahweh*. Most bibles today follow suit, using "LORD" in all caps as a substitute for *Yahweh*.

In Exodus 3:14, God closely associates *Yahweh* with the name *I AM*. It is a name disclosing God's inner nature. He alone is the uncreated Creator; everything else is the work of his hands.

After revealing his holy name, the Lord tells Moses to approach Pharaoh with a demand. Pharaoh is to let the Israelites go so they may worship God in the wilderness. As with so many kings and rulers in history, Pharaoh is infuriated by the Israelites' desire to worship the Lord. He says scornfully to Moses:

> Who is the LORD, that I should
> obey him and let Israel go?[12]

God's response is to turn the Nile to blood. Pharaoh had previously turned the Nile into a river of death when he ordered all newborn Israelite boys cast into its waters. In turning the Nile to blood, the Lord reveals and judges the monstrosity of Pharaoh's decree.

The blood-red Nile is the first of what will be ten plagues, a display of divine power on an unprecedented scale. The blood red Nile is followed by plagues of frogs and insects, disease, and boils. With every plague, the Lord intensifies the pressure on Pharaoh. The Egyptians had employed a strategy of crushing the Israelites with increasingly heavy burdens. Now that same measure is being measured onto them.[13]

With each plague, Pharaoh has the opportunity to relent and repent; his heart, however, only hardens. His response remains the scornful answer delivered earlier to Moses: *Who is the LORD, that I should obey him and let Israel go?*

The plagues are a shock and awe campaign against Pharaoh and the Egyptians to persuade them to free the Israelites. But the Bible also describes them as an execution of judgement against the Egyptian gods[14]—a salvo in what will be a long war between the Lord and the demon gods of the pagan world.

We're used to thinking of pagan deities as mythological, figments of the imagination. That's not the biblical view. We can't read the Bible correctly unless we understand that the pagan gods it mentions—the gods of the Egyptians, the Philistines, the Romans—are in fact demons;[15] fallen angels who rebelled against the Lord in heaven and continue that rebellion on earth.

The tactics and stratagems of that rebellion will vary in response to different historical and cultural contexts. A major tactic of the demons, however, especially in early epochs, is to falsely present themselves as "gods," revealing their preternatural gifts and terrorizing men and women into offering worship owed the Lord alone. As St. Justin Martyr, an early Christian apologist writing to the Roman emperor Antoninus Pius around 155 BC, explains:

> *From ancient times these evil demons, effecting apparitions of themselves . . . showed such fearful sights to men, that those who did not use their*

*reason ... and not knowing that these were demons
... called them gods.*[16]

The inspiring of false religions, leading men and women away from the knowledge and worship of the true God, is one of the earliest demonic deceptions. The plagues are meant in part to combat it. Through the plagues, the Lord unmasks the demons, reveals their empty promises, and casts them from their positions as "gods."

Each plague is a laser-like assault on the sphere of influence of a specific Egyptian deity. The plague of frogs, for example, attacks Heket, a fertility goddess depicted as a frog. The death of livestock is targeted at Hathor, the cow-goddess.

Early in the confrontation, the pagan gods answer God's miracles with prodigies of their own. God turns Moses' staff into a snake; the pagan magicians do the same. God turns the Nile red and sends a plague of frogs onto the land. Again, the magicians match him.

Then God ups the ante. He *creates*. From the dust of the earth, he creates a swarm of gnats. And the magicians are helpless to follow. After this, they go to Pharaoh and tell him, *This is the finger of God.*[17]

The Tenth Plague

Pharaoh's heart remains hardened through the plague of gnats and the hailstorms and locusts that follow. The ninth plague is the most terrible yet; three days of darkness so dense the Egyptians are unable to see each other, or even move. The plague awesomely demonstrates the power of the Lord and makes a mockery of the sun god Ra, chief of the Egyptian pantheon. Still, Pharaoh refuses to let the Israelites go.

After the ninth plague, the Lord is ready to bring the showdown to a close. He does so with a tenth and final plague that will take the life of every firstborn male among the Egyptians, man and beast alike.

Pharaoh had ordered the murder of all newborn boys among the Israelites. Now Pharaoh will be repaid in kind. The Lord tells Moses what he will do:

> On this same night I will go through Egypt, striking down every firstborn in the land, man and beast alike, and executing judgement on all the gods of Egypt.[18]

Before the sword of judgement falls, the Lord tells Moses to have every Israelite family sacrifice a lamb and mark their doorposts with its blood. The blood of the lamb saves the Israelites. During the night, the Lord will "pass over" their homes as he strikes down the Egyptian firstborn.

When the tenth plague takes Pharaoh's son and heir, Pharaoh finally admits defeat. He allows the Israelites to go.

Then he changes his mind. He *still* will not submit to the Lord. Instead, Pharaoh sends his soldiers and six hundred of his best chariots after the Israelites to kill them in the wilderness.

The Israelites seem trapped—the Red Sea before them and Pharaoh's fearsome army behind. Despite the devastation of the plagues, Pharaoh's six hundred war chariots are still the most powerful military force on earth.

Yet the Lord intervenes. First he holds the Egyptians at bay through a miraculous pillar of fire and cloud. Then he drives back the sea with a strong wind, making a kind of valley for the Israelites to pass through.

It must have been frightening. The Bible says the Israelites crossed during the night. Walls of water pulsed and roiled on either side, while behind were the six hundred war chariots of their enemy.

The Lord led every single one of the Israelites through the dark valley of water unscathed. In the morning, when the Egyptians pursued, the water crashed down upon the most powerful army on earth. Every one of Pharaoh's soldiers died.

This event, and the tenth plague and Passover that preceded it, was seared in the Israelites' memory forever. It is history's preeminent display of God's absolute power over the nations and their pagan gods. It is the proof and pledge of his ability to rescue his people.

Following the parting of the Red Sea, Moses and the people compose a hymn of praise. In calling for the Lord to reign forever, they acclaim him king.

> I will sing to the LORD, for he has
>   triumphed gloriously.
> Pharaoh's chariots and his host he
>   hurled into the sea;
> Who is like you, O LORD, among the
>   gods?
> Who is like you, majestic in
>   holiness,
> terrible in glorious deeds, doing
>   wonders?
> May the LORD reign forever and
>   ever![19]

This is the Israelites' first commemoration of the Exodus. In the centuries that follow, in both times of triumph and danger and defeat, they will recall it often.

The Psalms and later the prophets will remind Israel of the Exodus, pointing to it as evidence of God's power and willingness to save. By freeing the Israelites from Pharaoh, by preserving them from the dreadful plagues and parting the waters of the Red Sea, the Lord has demonstrated his might and trustworthiness. Israel must in turn keep its covenant with him.

Journey to Sinai

With the destruction of Pharaoh's army, the Lord liberates his people. After four centuries in Egypt, he intends to fulfill his promise to Abraham and bring them to Canaan, the promised land.

There is one stop first: a journey to his holy mountain, Sinai.

The location of Mount Sinai is one of the Bible's great mysteries. Though we no longer know precisely where Mount Sinai is, we do know what happened there.

The Lord came upon the mountain in smoke and fire. Earlier he had revealed himself to Moses in the burning bush. Now he reveals his power and majesty to all.

The Israelites' experience of God at Sinai is awesome and, frankly, terrifying.

The Israelites beg God never to appear to them again in such a manner. Surprisingly, the Lord praises the Israelites for this request, saying that what they ask is good. He promises the Israelites that instead of more Sinai experiences, he will one day raise up among them a prophet like Moses who will faithfully deliver his word.[20]

The Day of the Assembly

The Bible speaks repeatedly of the gathering at Sinai and calls it "the day of the assembly." In the Greek Old Testament, the Septuagint, the word for "assembly" is *ekklesia*. It's the same word the Greek New Testament will use to refer to the Church.

The day of the assembly is one of the most important days in Israel's history, commemorated in the Jewish feast day *Shavuot*. It is during the theophany on Sinai that God gives the Israelites his holy Law, the Torah. The tablets of the Ten Commandments are inscribed, the Bible says, by God's own finger.[21] In giving the Law to the Israelites, the Lord makes them *a kingdom of priests, a holy nation*—a people set apart for himself.[22]

Today we're accustomed to thinking of the Ten Commandments as a universal code of conduct, its demands *written on our hearts*.[23] It's easy to overlook how corrupt ancient societies were and what a distinctive standard of morality the Ten Commandments set.

The pagan nations surrounding Israel were built on religious and political systems that *required* violations of the Commandments. These nations were dedicated to demon gods, worshipped and appeased through graven images. Often these gods demanded murder, in the form of human sacrifice, and adultery, in the form of temple prostitution. The Law forbade these evil acts. It set the Israelites apart from those who practiced them.

The Mosaic law, however, is not simply about forbidding moral evil and enjoining what is universally good. Its ceremonial and dietary statutes impose distinctive, and sometimes seemingly arbitrary, practices upon the Israelites. Jewish dietary law, known as *kashrut,* is not a requirement of natural morality, nor does it have anything to do with food safety. So why does God command it?

My thoughts are not your thoughts, neither are your ways my ways.[24] We cannot know all God intends in establishing the Mosaic law—though as we will see, this will be a subject of contemplation for some of the great religious geniuses of history.

Yet this *effect* of the Mosaic law we can note: it shapes the Israelites as a people set apart, calls them to assembly, and shields them from assimilating with pagans.

God's setting his people apart had begun with his covenant with Abraham. By choosing circumcision as his covenant's sign, he had put up a kind of barrier to mingling and intermarriage with pagans. In addition, the pain of adult circumcision had the effect of dissuading all but the most determined converts.

This protective barrier was raised higher still with the Mosaic law. The dietary statutes, the Sabbath regulations, religious laws requiring sacrifice only at the Tabernacle or Temple; these served to keep the Israelites distinctive, protected, enclosed. The Law reminded the Israelites daily of their consecration at Sinai. It was a continual call from the Lord to repudiate any desire to return to the *flesh pots of Egypt*[25] or conform to pagan ways.

The Lord is My Shepherd

The Lord had freed his people from Pharaoh and given them his Law. He had shown his might and holiness. Before arriving at Canaan, there is another Divine attribute they must learn and come to rely on: his steadfast love.

The image of God as shepherd recurs often in the Bible. Jesus calls himself the Good Shepherd,[26] and David famously addresses God as shepherd in Psalm 23. This shepherd image for God originates in the Exodus and Israel's wandering in the desert. First, God parts the Red Sea for the Israelites, and the rod of Moses is their comfort as they cross the valley of the shadow of death. Then God shepherds them in the wilderness.

He feeds them with quail and manna, the mysterious bread from heaven; he provides them with life-giving water through a rock that accompanies them, which Moses must strike; he heals them from snakebite. His pillar of cloud and fire stays with them, leading them, lighting their path, shielding them from the sun.

The prophet Isaiah and the Psalms both refer to God as a shepherd to Israel during this period. The Psalms tells us *he led forth his people like sheep, and guided them in the wilderness like a flock.*[27]

God is not distant from the Israelites; after his mighty works, he does not leave them orphans.[28] He quite literally dwells among them in the tent or Tabernacle housing the Ark of the Covenant—the golden chest enclosing the tablets of the Ten Commandments.

The Ark of the Covenant is the national treasure of the Israelites. At Sinai they had been nearly overcome with fear and dread when they had seen the glory of the Lord. Yet now the Lord remains with them in a quieter way, accompanying them in his own tent, the Tabernacle, in their wanderings through the wilderness.

During this time, the Lord was teaching the Israelites that he is holy, and merciful, and *reliable*, even when he seemed to delay, even against seemingly insurmountable odds. He was building, and testing, their trust.

It was a test they frequently failed.

Wandering in the Wilderness

The Bible provides several examples of the Israelites failure to trust. One is their storing of manna, the bread from heaven which the Lord sends like the dewfall each morning.

Hundreds of years earlier, God had fed his people and preserved them from famine by inspiring Joseph to store up in Egypt a seven-year supply of grain. Now he wants to provide in a more intimate way. The Lord wants the Israelites to gather their manna each morning, to rely on him *to give us this day our daily bread.*[29]

He forbids their storing of manna, with the

exception of the eve of the Sabbath when they are to gather a two-day supply. Some of the Israelites fail the test. They store their manna, keep it overnight, and wake to find it stinking and crawling with worms.[30]

The Book of Numbers records another test. God orders the Israelites to send twelve men, one from each of the tribes, into Canaan as spies. They are a reconnaissance team scouting the terrain and local populace before the Israelites enter the Promised Land *en masse*.

When the spies return, they are crestfallen; the Promised Land is already inhabited, including by giants. The spies have seen God rescue and free the Israelites from the most powerful military on earth, Egypt. Yet now they lose their resolve and urge retreat.

Only two of the spies, Caleb from the tribe of Judah and Joshua from Ephraim, part of the house of Joseph, keep their resolve. They try to restore the flagging spirits of the Israelites.[31]

> If the LORD is pleased with us, he
>   will bring us into the land. Don't
>   be afraid of the people . . . the
>   LORD is with us!

In response, the Israelites threaten to stone

Caleb and Joshua. Then the Lord intervenes. He comes upon the Israelites in glory and pronounces judgement on their lack of trust.

The Lord decrees he will now delay the entry of the Israelites into the Promised Land. The current generation will spend the next forty years wandering in the wilderness.[32]

> Of all the people who have seen my glory, the signs I did in Egypt and in the wilderness... not one shall see the land which I promised.

Children and youth under the age of twenty are exempted from this punishment, as are Joshua and Caleb. Interestingly, generations later it is the tribes of Joshua and Caleb—Judah and Ephraim—who will rule over the others.

God's punishment of the Israelites for their lack of trust seems harsh. Yet he was forming and forging the people of his covenant for generations of trials ahead. Trust in him was required for his people to survive. Absolute trust would be crucial for his covenant to come to fruition.

The Time of the Judges

A generation after leaving Egypt, the Israelites arrive in Canaan, now to be known as Israel. Joshua and Caleb are the only members of their generation who enter. Even Moses failed to trust the Lord perfectly. When the Lord tells Moses to obtain water, not by striking the rock as he had in the past, but by speaking to it, Moses disobeys. He strikes the rock again, and in consequence, he is denied entrance to Canaan.[33]

The Israelites have now arrived in the land promised to Abraham hundreds of years before. For several generations, they will live there with the Lord himself as their king.

This is the time of the Judges; and despite battles, and setbacks, and sin, it is a time of joy and hope, for God has rescued his people and dwells among them still, enthroned between the two cherubim of the Ark:

> The LORD is king, the peoples
>   tremble;
> he is enthroned on the
>   cherubim, the earth quakes.
> Great is the LORD in Zion,
> exalted above all the peoples.

> Let them praise your great and
> awesome name!³⁴

The period of the Judges is an interesting one in Jewish history. It is not a messianic age. The Israelites are still trying to claim and hold on to their country. There is too much fighting for it to be that.

It is, however, a special time, because the memory of the rescue from Egypt and God's revealing himself in the events of the Exodus and the theophany at Sinai are very fresh. The Israelites are no longer oppressed by Pharaoh or any human king. The promise God made to Abraham hundreds of years earlier, to give them the land of Canaan, is fulfilled before their eyes. Above all, the Lord dwells with them in incredible intimacy in the Tabernacle housing the Ark of the Covenant.

The Israelites face challenges during the period of the Judges. They are in some ways the same challenges faced during the wandering in the wilderness. The Israelites must trust God to keep his word, even when he delays, even when, humanly speaking, his promises seem impossible to fulfill. And they must keep themselves holy by following the Law, separating themselves from the sins and demonic idolatry of their neighbors.

Their relationship with God is absolutely unique among the nations. They have to do all in their power to defend, protect, and preserve it.

Thus the Jewish people became a nation through the events of the Exodus. And for hundreds of years, during the period of the Judges, their only king was the Lord.

In many ways, that first divine king of the Israelites cannot help but remind us of Jesus. Like Jesus, the Lord miraculously fed his people, giving them manna, bread, in the wilderness. The Lord brought them to a mountain to teach them. He shepherded, taught, and healed them. He dwelt among them in a Tabernacle.

The Lord rebuked and cast out demons, the so-called "gods" of Egypt. He referred to himself as "I AM." He demanded holiness and required his people to distinguish themselves from the practices of their pagan neighbors.

Still, there was this crucial difference: When confronted with a hostile power, Pharaoh, the Lord had triumphed over him with overwhelming power. Jesus, in contrast, had stood before Pilate as a severely beaten prisoner. At the pivotal moment,

Jesus presents himself as powerless, meek as a lamb.

During the time of the Judges, the Israelites cultivated the land they had been promised, the Lord dwelling in their midst. As time passed, they began to envy the human kings of their pagan neighbors. The Israelites wanted a human king too, with an army to defend them. They did not want to rely day by day, moment by moment, on the Lord.

Their desire was a sin. It would ultimately lead to nearly one thousand years of suffering. Yet for a time, they *would* have a glorious king, a man after the Lord's own heart—a ruler whose royal line would produce the Messiah.

2

DAVID

A MAN AFTER GOD'S OWN HEART

For several hundred years, after escaping Pharaoh, Israel stood alone among the nations in having no king but the Lord.

As he had done in Egypt and in the wanderings in the wilderness, God often proved his power to save. He gave victories to the female judge Deborah over the Canaanite general Sisera and to Gideon and his army of three hundred men. He miraculously strengthened Samson against the Philistines.

When the Israelites worshipped the Lord and kept his Law, they were invincible. When they succumbed to the enticements of pagan gods, they were defeated and enslaved ... until they repented and the Lord rescued them again.

Eventually the Israelites wearied of miracles.

They went to the prophet Samuel and demanded God give them a king to rule and lead them in battle.

This request was a sin, a lack of trust in God. It would have consequences. God warned the Israelites earthly kings would oppress them and take their children and wealth.

Yet, in a mysterious way, the establishment of a human king was part of God's plan. God told Moses the Israelites might one day desire a king, and they could have one—provided it was a king chosen by God.[1]

Of all the kings in the Old Testament, none was more clearly chosen by God than David. The Bible calls him a man after the Lord's own heart.[2]

Not only would David offer the royal bloodline for the Messiah; he would also provide an unforgettable image of the kind of man God desired for his chosen king.

DAVID WAS NOT the first king of Israel. That position belonged to Saul. As with so many of Israel's leaders, Saul lost favor with God for failing to trust and obey.

When he was first anointed by the prophet Samuel, Saul seemed poised to become an excellent king. The Bible calls him the handsomest man among the Israelites, standing head and shoulders above everyone else.[3]

His looks and stature did not make Saul boastful or puff him up with pride. When Samuel tells Saul he'll be king, Saul demurs, pointing to his modest lineage and membership in the tribe of Benjamin, smallest of the twelve tribes.[4]

As king, though, Saul will sin by not relying totally on the Lord. On one occasion, he is on the battlefield, delaying his attack until Samuel comes and offers sacrifice. Samuel is late, and Saul's army begins to desert. Saul rashly makes the sacrifice himself, usurping Samuel's role and presuming to come before the Lord not only as king but as priest.

Saul's impatience and lack of trust cost him his kingdom. Just as he finishes making the offering, Samuel arrives. *What have you done!* Samuel exclaims. *Now your kingdom shall not endure.*[5]

Saul's disobedience paves the way for David. After God removes his anointing from Saul, he sends Samuel to Bethlehem, to a man named Jesse, to anoint one of his sons.[6]

This is the One!

The account of Samuel's anointing of David is a great contrast to the anointing of Saul. When Samuel arrives at Jesse's home in Bethlehem, he sees his son Eliab, a man of *lofty stature* as Saul had been. Samuel thinks this must be the one, but God rejects Eliab. God will not choose Israel's king by appearances. He will look into the heart.

Seven sons of Jesse are presented to Samuel, but none of them are the one God has chosen. He asks Jesse, *Are these all the sons you have?*

Jesse then calls his youngest son, David, in from the fields where he has been tending sheep. As soon as he enters, the Lord immediately tells Samuel, *This is the one!*

In later life, we know David sins greatly. He sins through his adultery with Bathsheba. He sins through the arranged killing of her husband, Uriah.[7] And he sins by conducting a census without paying a census tax or "ransom" as required by the Lord.[8] A census is a tool for kings to tax and draft their subjects. The Israelites had been set apart for the Lord. They were *his* flock, whom Israel's king was to care for, not fleece.

Still, God describes David as "a man after my own heart." It is one of the highest accolades given to a human being in the Bible. It is given to David, despite his sins, because of his compassion, his praise, his trust.

What makes David a man after God's own heart? In Acts 13:22, we get the answer: *He will carry out my every wish.* Of course, this isn't literally true of David. David is a sinner. It will only be a later *son* of David who can say, truthfully, *I **always** do what is pleasing to him.*[9]

Still, David is one of the most outstanding examples we have in the Bible of a man who trusts in the Lord. Despite lapses, David habitually waits on the Lord, waits for God to unfold his plan.

Nowhere is David's trust more evident than in his famous battle with Goliath, champion of the Philistines, a nation at war with Israel. David visits the battlefield in the Valley of Elah, bringing supplies to his brothers. He is outraged when he hears Goliath's taunts. He volunteers to face Goliath himself.

Saul tells David he is too young. David insists. As a teenage shepherd, he has already risked his life for his flock, killing a lion and bear. Goliath has insulted God, says David; he will deal Goliath a similar fate.

The Bible tells us about the battle in 1 Samuel 17. One of the first things we learn is how enormous Goliath is, nearly ten feet tall, fully armored, with a spear and a sword to match.

Goliath is the champion of the Philistines. He derisively challenges the Israelites, calling upon them to produce a warrior who will face him in single combat. The Israelite soldiers are terrified. Not one takes up the challenge.

David arrives, outraged that this pagan, *this uncircumcised Philistine* as he calls him, is mocking God's people. As is so often the case with David, he is not personally insulted, but he's passionately protective of the Lord's glory.

David approaches Goliath unarmored, with a sling and five smooth stones.

Later readers will see significance in the number. In David's encounter with Goliath, they cannot help but see another King, and another Shepherd. He, stripped of his garments, will confront the ancient enemy of God's people armed with nothing but five precious wounds.

Goliath is astonished when David approaches him. He mocks David, promising to feed his body to the birds. David responds:

> You come against me with sword
> and spear and scimitar, but I
> come against you in the name of
> the LORD.

Then David slings a stone at Goliath, fells him

with a single shot, and slices off his head with Goliath's own sword.

Meek and Humble of Heart

After vanquishing Goliath, David is a national hero. Saul gives David his daughter, Michal, in marriage and appoints him commander over all his forces. David goes from victory to victory. His soldiers love him, and the women of Israel acclaim him in song. *Saul has slain his thousands*, they sing, *David his tens of thousands.*[10]

David's popularity threatens Saul. He is the king still, but David is clearly the Lord's anointed. God has chosen David to be king and found a dynasty once Saul dies.

Saul's admiration for David and gratitude to him gives way to jealousy. That David now has what was once Saul's, the Lord's anointing, drives Saul nearly mad. Saul plots David's death in battle, hoping to use the Philistines to do his dirty work. In his madness, he even casts his spear at David, making his own direct attempt on David's life.[11]

Saul's jealousy and violence towards David is in stark contrast with the behavior of his own son and heir, Jonathan. Jonathan loves David. He gives David his own cloak and clothing, symbolically acknowledging David will be Israel's next king. As

John the Baptist will do, Jonathan points without jealousy to the Lord's anointed and proclaims, *This man is greater than me.*[12]

While David manages to escape Saul's plots and spear, Saul's jealousy only deepens. Eventually David flees for his life. At no time does he strike back at Saul, though he has opportunities. Despite being persecuted, he is loyal to Israel's king for years.

Saul pursues David relentlessly, chasing David with his army from place to place. The Bible presents us with one account where Saul gets so close that David is able to sneak up while Saul is sleeping and cut some cloth from his robe. In another account, David steals a spear and jug of water from Saul's side.[13]

David is showing Saul that he could kill him if he wanted. Yet David will not strike back. He will not come to the throne with Saul's blood staining his hands. Instead, he shows Saul mercy and compassion. He provides a powerful example of *praying for those who persecute you.*[14]

Finally, Saul sees he's been a fool. He repents and acknowledges David will succeed him as king.

David and Saul reconcile, but David does not return to Saul's palace; he and a loyal retinue live in exile during the remainder of Saul's reign. Soon Saul and several of his sons, including Jonathan, are killed in battle against the Philistines. David grieves deeply, magnanimously overlooking Saul's personal vendetta against him and his many flaws.

After the death of Saul, the tribe of Judah anoints David king. The Bible tells us that David is thirty years old when he receives this second anointing and begins his kingship.[15] It is the same age Jesus will begin his public ministry.[16]

Israel continues to be ruled by a surviving son of Saul, Ishbosheth, and for a time, there is war between Israel and Judah. Then Ishbosheth is murdered. David is anointed a third and final time, this time as king of all Israel, uniting the twelve tribes.

The nation is about to enter its Golden Age.

Jerusalem: City of the King

David becomes king of all Israel during a period of intense warfare with the Philistines. Despite his earlier triumph over Goliath, and his spectacular victories as a military captain for Saul, the Philistines have remained a fierce and determined foe.

David will rout the Philistines soon after coming to the throne. Yet before recounting David's campaign against the Philistines, or any other kingly deeds, the Bible tells us of his encounter with another foe, the Jebusites, and the conquest of their capital, Jerusalem. It will be one of David's most lasting accomplishments as king.

By the time of David, the Israelites have been in the Promised Land for several generations. In different campaigns, under different leaders and judges, they have increased their holdings. They have faced the peoples that so terrified their ancestors and caused them to retreat after Moses sent Joshua and Caleb and the other spies to scout the land.

When the Israelites rely on the Lord, they win their battles, making the land of Canaan the land of Israel city by city, town by town. Jerusalem, however, has not been conquered. The city, and the mountain fortress at its core, *Zion*, enjoy an aura of impregnability. When David and his men go to Jerusalem to claim it, the Jebusites boast behind their ramparts, *The blind and the lame will drive you away!*[17]

The Jebusites' taunt implies their fortifications are too strong to be breached, even if those manning the walls are blind and lame. Later readers will see another meaning. They will remember another King, a son of David who will come to Jerusalem and encounter the blind and lame, not as foe, but as savior and friend—whose gift to them will put in motion the plot to have him killed.[18]

The Jebusite taunt fails as a prophecy against David. He avoids the trap of a frontal assault. David and his men enter the city stealthily through a tunnel carrying water to the city. He conquers Jerusalem and makes Zion his home.

For the first time, Jerusalem is in Israelite hands. Yet this is not the first time God's people have been at this spot. Jerusalem has already played a significant role in salvation history. That is why David's heart burns for Jerusalem, and why he is determined to make Zion his home.

In becoming king of Jerusalem, David associates himself and his dynasty with one of the most mysterious figures of the Bible, Melchizedek. We read about Melchizedek in Genesis chapter 14. The Bible introduces Melchizedek as a king, the king of Jerusalem, or *Salem* as it's originally called; yet he is also a priest. Melchizedek blesses Abraham and offers a sacrifice of bread and wine. It is a priestly sacrifice we will not see offered again until the Last Supper.

Melchizedek's priesthood is *sui generis*, unlinked with the hereditary Levitical priesthood which develops later. The Bible tells us nothing of Melchizedek's ancestors or descendants. Melchizedek appears as an almost divine figure, *having neither beginning of days nor end of life*, as the Epistle to the Hebrews notes.[19] In Psalm 110, a Psalm we will consider again, David addresses the future Messiah as *a priest forever in the order of Melchizedek*.[20]

Melchizedek's offering of bread and wine is the first sacrifice the Bible records in Jerusalem. Another soon follows: the binding of Isaac. It is there on Mount Zion that Abraham prepares to sacrifice Isaac to the Lord, until an angel stops him. It is there on Mount Zion that Abraham tells Isaac, *God himself will provide the sacrifice*.[21]

In Genesis, Mount Zion is called Mount Moriah. Abraham names it *Yahweh-yireh*, meaning "the Lord will provide."[22]

According to Jewish tradition, it is also on Mount Zion where Isaac's son Jacob has his famous dream of a ladder uniting heaven and earth.[23] It is a dream that both recalls Abraham's act of worship and sacrifice and hints at other acts of sacrifice to come.

One of those acts is made by David himself. It is after David conducts his census in defiance of the Lord. In response to David's sin, the Lord sends a plague upon Israel. In three days, about seventy thousand people die. Yet the Lord relents and extends to Israel his divine mercy when David repents and offers a sacrifice of oxen on Zion. *Then the Lord answered his prayer for the land, and the plague upon Israel was stopped.*[24]

Your Son will Build My Temple

David is drawn to Jerusalem, as will be so many rulers and generals in the years ahead. Some, like the Queen of Sheba and Alexander the Great, will come to encounter God. Others will come to taunt and defy him.

Both groups, good and wicked, are driven by the intuition that in Jerusalem, the Lord of hosts is present in a special way.

When David brings Israel's greatest treasure, the Ark of the Covenant, to Jerusalem, he is nearly delirious with joy. He leads a magnificent procession for the Ark and dances before it with such abandon his wife, Michal, complains he has demeaned himself. David makes no apology. As is so typical of him, David cares little for his dignity, desiring only to love the Lord with all his heart, mind, and soul.

During the wandering in the wilderness and later the time of the Judges, the Ark moved with the Israelites from place to place, traveling with them even into battle. Now that his kingdom is secure, David wants the Ark to have a permanent home and proposes to build it a house, a Temple, in Jerusalem.

The Lord has a different plan. He conveys it to David through the prophet Nathan:

> When your days have been
> completed and you rest with
> your ancestors, I will raise up
> your offspring after you, sprung
> from your loins, and I will
> establish his kingdom. He it
> is who shall build a house for
> my name, and I will establish his
> royal throne forever. I will be a
> father to him, and he shall be a
> son to me.[25]

Nathan's prophecy is known to Bible scholars as the *Dynastic Oracle*. It is God's covenant with David, a man after his own heart, that his house or dynasty will last forever. It expands and specifies the earlier prophecy of Jacob that *the scepter will not depart from Judah ...until Shiloh comes*. God had promised lasting sovereignty to Judah; now he promises everlasting sovereignty to David's son. God promises more: David's son will build a house for God, and God will be a father to him.

David's son and successor, Solomon, fulfills

these promises in part. Solomon builds a house for God, the great Temple, right on Mount Zion. It is built on the very spot where Abraham bound Isaac and Jacob dreamed of a ladder between heaven and earth.

Yet Solomon cannot be called the "son of God" in any unique or extraordinary sense. And his reign had a definite end. In its fullest sense, the Dynastic Oracle is left to be fulfilled not by Solomon but by another son of David, the Messiah.

After hearing God promise *your house and kingdom are firm forever*,[26] David is filled with thanksgiving. Later he will celebrate God's promise in Psalm 110, exulting at what God has promised his descendant: to place him at his right hand forever, and make him invincible against his enemies.

> The LORD says to my lord:
> "Sit at my right hand,
> while I make your enemies your
>   footstool."...
> The LORD extends your strong
>   scepter from Zion.
> Have dominion over your
>   enemies![27]

The Psalm is one Israel will hold fast to in the generations ahead. One thousand years later, Jesus will quote it,[28] asking his listeners to reflect upon the mysteries within.

In the reigns of David and Solomon, we see present, though imperfectly, various aspects of the kingdom of the Messiah. First, David and Solomon are both anointed kings who end their reigns ruling over all twelve tribes of Israel. None of their merely human successors will ever do the same.

They ascend their thrones in the City of David, Jerusalem. David of course is already king when he comes to Jerusalem. His kingship, however, manifests itself in stage—and reaches its fullness when he mounts his throne in Jerusalem.

Both David and Solomon are zealous for the house of the Lord, which David yearns for and Solomon builds. Both offer sacrifice on Zion.

Neither David nor Solomon have an everlasting reign. They each, however, rule for forty years. Forty is the number of a biblical generation. By ruling for an entire generation, they show a certain completeness, prefiguring the one who will have an everlasting throne.

During the reigns of David and then Solomon, Israel is wealthy, populous, and militarily strong. It achieves the status of a world power, which it will never reach again. The Queen of Sheba comes all the way from Ethiopia to visit Solomon; she is not the only world leader to do so. The Bible tells us *the whole world sought audience with Solomon, to hear the wisdom God had put into his heart.*[29]

This moment when Israel is capable of being *a light unto the nations* is lost after Solomon. But the memory of it, and the desire for it, live on in expectations for the Messiah. Prophets such as Isaiah will proclaim it as a hallmark of his reign.[30]

Man of Prayer

In so many ways David serves as a type for the Messiah. Christian kings and emperors throughout the ages would take David as a model too—sometimes, as in the case of Charlemagne, even using "David" as a title or pseudonym.

The Middle Ages ranked David among the "Nine Worthies," a group of princes from literature, history, and the Bible who exemplify the ideals of chivalry.[31] Themes, events, and parallels from David's life are present in the Arthurian legends, with the great knight Galahad, finder of the Holy Grail, bearing King David's sword.

History remembers David as a model king. Yet it honors him daily for something still greater: being a man of prayer.

David was a gifted musician. As a youth, he

had soothed King Saul and lifted his spirits with song. As a man, David poured out his soul and lifted it to God with the Psalms.

David's Psalms express a wide range of emotions and spiritual states: praise, sorrow, contrition, and above all, trust. Shakespeare is often praised as a universal writer (*He was not for an age, but for all time!*[32]), yet this acclamation belongs first, and all the more strongly, to David. While David draws deeply in the Psalms from the events of his own life, he speaks for all who have ever repented, sorrowed, struggled, and praised. Above all, he speaks as a man after God's own heart.

David's prayers, the Psalms, enabled Israel to lift its voice to God through the centuries. They became, with others that were added later, the prayer book of Israel. Jesus was steeped in the Psalms; he quotes from the Psalms more than any other book in the Bible.[33] The Psalms remain essential to Christian prayer today, woven into the Mass and at the heart of the Divine Office, the daily prayer of the Church.

Of the Bible's 150 Psalms, 76 list David as author. New Testament writers attribute a few additional Psalms to David as well. Several Psalms list biographical details from David's life, such as Psalm 51, in which David begs God to *blot out my offence,* his sin with Bathsheba, and offers the sacrifice of *a humbled, contrite heart.*

Perhaps no Psalm is more expressive of David, of his unshakeable trust in God, than his beloved Psalm 23.

> The LORD is my shepherd, I shall
>   not want;
> he makes me lie down in green
>   pastures.
> He leads me beside still waters;
> he restores my soul.
> He leads me in paths of
>   righteousness
> for his name's sake.
> Even though I walk through the
>   valley of the shadow of death,
> I fear no evil;
> for you are with me;
> Your rod and your staff,
> they comfort me.[34]

In a few short verses, we hear the memory of David's time spent shepherding the flocks of his father, Jesse, in Bethlehem. We hear his marveling about how the Lord protected him from his enemies and perhaps an allusion to his fight with Goliath in the Valley of Elah, where

David went forth confidently in the shadow of death.

As David must have, we remember the Israelites who were shepherded by God after the Exodus and led safely through the Red Sea—the walls of water forming another kind of "valley of death." And coming after David, we cannot help but hear the hope of later Israelites who would pray this Psalm, Israelites living in exile in Assyria or Babylon, trusting that the Lord will lead them home.

For Christians, Psalm 23 is above all a reminder of the Good Shepherd, Jesus. One thousand years after David, Jesus will give himself this title and promise to remain with his flock always—even through the valley of the shadow of death.[35]

AT THE HEIGHT of Solomon's reign, Israel was a nation like no other. In the span of two generations, this people set apart had gone from struggling and besieged to a world power—admired, respected, prosperous, secure.

No longer was Israel taunted and mocked, as Saul and his soldiers had been by the giant Goliath. Now Solomon's counsel was sought by the whole world, and kings and queens came to pay him homage.

It was a shining moment in Israel's history, and it began with the boy, David, pulling Goliath's sword from its scabbard in victory after striking him with a stone.

This shining moment was all too brief. Solomon married or took as concubines hundreds of foreign women and brought their idols into his household. His lust would lead Israel away from the Lord. It allowed the pagan gods the Lord had judged so powerfully in Egypt to regain a foothold among the Israelites and corrupt them again.

Under Solomon's son and successor, Rehoboam, the kingdom of Israel would be split in two. Long centuries of suffering would begin.

Yet Israel would never lose the memory of its days of glory. It would never forget its shepherd king, David, a man after God's own heart, whose songs, the Psalms, were the prayer of the nation.

It would never forget God's covenant with the house of David.

And it would cling to the promise of a future king, a son of David who would also be a son to God, and whose royal throne would last forever.

3

EXILE

BY THE WATERS OF BABYLON

In 586 BC, some four centuries after David, his descendant Zedekiah was thrust before the man who'd just invaded Jerusalem: the king of Babylon, Nebuchadnezzar.

Nebuchadnezzar had conquered Jerusalem once before. Eleven years earlier, he'd dethroned Zedekiah's predecessor and nephew, Jeconiah. He'd force-marched Jeconiah and thousands of Judah's most prominent citizens to Babylon; made Zedekiah his vassal; and extorted crippling tribute payments—a ransom for the safety of the Judahite captives.

When Zedekiah rebelled, Nebuchadnezzar invaded Jerusalem again. Then he turned to Zedekiah.

Nebuchadnezzar had Zedekiah's sons slain

before him. Next he ordered Zedekiah's eyes gouged out, ensuring the last images seen by Zedekiah would be the murder of his children.

Nebuchadnezzar loaded Zedekiah with chains. Then he sent the last king of Judah to join the earlier captives in Babylon, in current day Iraq.

His final outrage was reserved for the Temple. This holiest of sites—which Solomon had built and David had longed for, which Abraham had anticipated through his offering of Isaac at that very spot—Nebuchadnezzar ordered burned to the ground.[1]

This is how the history books tell us the house of David lost its throne. God had promised David a descendant who would build his Temple and rule forever. Now the Temple was gone and David's kingdom shattered, never to be reestablished in the same fashion.

The Babylonian Captivity is one of the bitterest times in Jewish history, a seventy-year reversal of the triumphs of the Exodus and of David and Solomon. It is the chief woe in a period of successive age-old sorrows: scattering, slavery, exile, defeat.

Yet this is also a period when expectations for the Messiah began to sharpen. Despite the darkness around them, the prophets point repeatedly to a light: a coming son of David, a true servant of the Lord, who will gather his people, conquer their enemies, free them from oppression, and build a Temple that will never be destroyed.

WHEN SOLOMON DIED the pain of the Babylonian exile was still hundreds of years in the future. A foretaste of it, however, was about to begin. The unity of God's people was broken almost immediately by Solomon's son and successor, Rehoboam.

Solomon had levied heavy taxes and work obligations on his people to construct the Temple, as well as for royal palaces and buildings. After Solomon died, and before Rehoboam was crowned, representatives of the twelve tribes came to see him.

The delegation promised loyalty to Rehoboam on one condition: that he lighten the tax burden his father Solomon had imposed and ease their yoke.

Rehoboam's reply was reckless in its harshness. It fulfilled the Lord's earlier warning to Israel that any king would seek to enslave them.

> My father made your yoke heavy,
> but I will make it heavier. My

> father beat you with whips, but I
> will beat you with scorpions.[2]

Rehoboam's reply led the ten northern tribes to revolt. The unity David achieved with his charisma and generosity was squandered by his grandson. The united monarchy ruling all Israel lasted just three generations.

The story of God's people would now play out within two nations: the kingdom of Israel in the north and the kingdom of Judah in the south.

A Nation Torn

The kingdom of Israel is established in 930 BC. Its first king is Jeroboam, who is *not* descended from David. David's line continues only in the smaller kingdom of Judah, comprised primarily of just two tribes, Judah and Benjamin.

It is difficult to overemphasize the tragedy of this diminishment of David's kingdom. These people, the twelve tribes, are meant to be one. They are children of Abraham, descendants of the patriarchs. They came out of Egypt together and had been set apart by God's law and his presence dwelling among them. The Lord had made clear his plan for the twelve tribes on the day of the assembly at Sinai: *You shall be a kingdom of priests and a holy nation.*[3]

Yet, in a mysterious way, this rupturing of the kingdom is part of God's providence too. The Bible makes that clear: First Kings chapter 12 tells us that *it is I*—that is, God—*who have brought this about.*

God's splitting of the kingdom is a punishment for Solomon's idolatry.[4] It is also, perhaps, a reward to Ephraim, Jeroboam's tribe. Ephraim is part of the house of Joseph. It is also the tribe of Joshua. Joshua and Caleb, from the tribe of Judah, were the only two out of twelve spies ready to trust the Lord and enter the Promised Land. Their two tribes are now the royal ones among the twelve.

The rupturing of David's kingdom is not meant to be permanent. *I will humble David's line* for the idolatry of Solomon, says the Lord, *but not forever*. The Lord wants Israel united, but not now; not when idolatry is practiced, and not under a man like Rehoboam and the many disappointing kings Judah will produce. Unification will come, but under a different set of circumstances and a far better king.

The history of the northern kingdom of Israel is brief, lasting roughly two hundred years. It is also tumultuous. During these two centuries, the kingdom of Israel will establish *nine* different dynasties. Each is founded on revolt and murder, the new king ascending by attacking the old.

The contrast with David is stark. None of the kings of Israel are men after God's own heart. Not one is good.

And not one avoids idolatry.

After Solomon built the Temple and installed the Ark within it, the Temple is the one place where the sacrifices called for in the Law of Moses can be made, the one dwelling where the Lord has *put his name*.

> You shall seek out the place which the LORD, your God, will choose from among all your tribes to put his name and make his dwelling there. There you shall go, bringing your offerings and sacrifices.[5]

When the northern tribes lose access to the Temple, they are unable to make the sacrifices required by the Mosaic law. They fall quickly into paganism, adopting the idolatrous practices of neighboring peoples. Some fall to the very depths, burning their own children alive in sacrifice to Baal.[6] The child sacrifices are an image of hell on earth—an assault by demons in the guise of "gods."

As a "people set apart," the Israelites had flourished, secure in the blessings of the Lord. In abandoning true worship of God and adopting idolatrous practices, they forsook that blessing. The consequences would be disastrous.

Within two hundred years of its founding, the kingdom of Israel is reduced to a vassal state of Assyria, a cruel and despotic empire that imposes enormous tributes or ransoms on its vassals. When Israel rebels, Assyria attacks. It deports many of Israel's leading citizens and installs a puppet king, Hoshea.

Then Hoshea rebels too. Assyria attacks again, captures Hoshea, and institutes another wave of forced deportations. By 722 BC, the kingdom of Israel comes to an end.

The Ten Lost Tribes

The captives are sent to Assyria in modern day Iraq. The Book of Tobit paints a somber picture of their captivity. Though a few occasionally find favor with the Assyrian kings, life for them is precarious, with hunger, poverty, and execution by their foreign masters a constant threat.

The Assyrian exile puts an end to the kingdom

of Israel as a political entity. Perhaps even more importantly, it initiates the scattering, or *diaspora,* of the ten northern tribes.

These ten "lost tribes of Israel" had been set apart by God, together with the tribes of Judah and Benjamin, as heirs to the promise of Abraham. Now, in forsaking the Temple and adopting pagan ways, they had weakened their identity. With the exiling to Assyria, they lose it altogether, disappearing almost entirely from history.

The fate of the ten lost tribes has fascinated many. The Bible doesn't tell us explicitly what happened to them. This has opened the way for all sorts of fantastic claims, such as that the tribes emigrated to Japan, or the British Isles, or even, some two thousand years before Columbus, to North America.

Many of these claims have no scientific or historical basis. They often arise out of a nationalistic or cultural misreading of the Bible—a desire to appropriate the status of God's chosen people by some later group.

We don't know everything that happened to the ten northern tribes, but we do know some things. First, not all the Israelites were deported. Some fled to the kingdom of Judah. Others were allowed to stay behind, often intermarrying with their foreign conquerors. Their descendants are the Samaritans we read about in the New Testament.

Of those who were deported, many adopted the practices of their conquerors and lost their distinctive identity through assimilation. Others preserved at least a memory of the Mosaic covenant, maintaining diaspora communities in the Assyrian Empire and eventually elsewhere as well.

Jerusalem Rescued

Twenty years after Assyria conquered Israel, the Assyrian Empire set its sights upon the kingdom of Judah—home to the house of David and the remnants of Israel's tribes.

Judah, like the kingdom of Israel before it, had been reduced to a vassal state of Assyria. When the Assyrian king Sargon II died on campaign, Judah as well as other regional states declared independence.

The new king, Sennacherib, gathered a massive army in response. Then he set forth. He would crush the rebels, plunder their treasure, and so terrorize the survivors that they would never dream of freedom again.

In his campaign against Judah, Sennacherib captured every fortified city except the capital,

Jerusalem. When the town of Lachish resisted, he laid siege. He breached its walls with battering rams, slaughtered anyone who resisted, and took the others as slaves.

As his army and wailing captives left the ruined city, he ordered the town leaders brought forth. Then he ordered them stripped naked, impaled or flayed alive,[7] and left writhing like insects outside the walls.

Finally, Sennacherib turned to what he most desired: Jerusalem. He prepared a siege as he had at Lachish, coiling his army like a monstrous serpent around the city.

Sennacherib taunted God's people as had Goliath and Pharaoh before him. His captain spoke on his behalf. He demanded that Jerusalem surrender, shouting at the men, women, and children behind Jerusalem's walls:

> Has any of the gods of the nations
>   ever rescued his land from the
>   power of the king of Assyria? ...
> Will the LORD then rescue
> Jerusalem from my power?[8]

Unlike the kings of Israel, the king of Judah, Hezekiah, remained faithful to the Lord. He prayed for deliverance, and the Lord heard. During the night, an angel struck down 185,000 Assyrian soldiers, prompting Sennacherib to abandon the siege and slink home.

Jerusalem Falls

The miraculous rescue from Sennacherib was a reprieve for Judah and a reward for faithfulness. Yet even Judah's faithfulness would not endure. While Judah had its good kings and periods of reform, it, too, would ultimately embrace immorality, covetousness, and above all, idolatry. As it had for Israel, Judah's disobedience would lead to destruction.

In 586 BC, just 136 years after the kingdom of Israel was annihilated, Judah suffers the same fate, falling not to Assyria but to Babylon and its king, Nebuchadnezzar. Just as the Israelites had been marched away in captivity, so the Judahites are now made captive too, exiled far away to Babylon in modern Iraq.

The conquest of the kingdom of Israel by Assyria and the exiling of its citizens had been a devastating blow to God's people. The conquest of Judah by Babylon 136 years later is worse. Only Judah's kings are descended from David. When the last king of Judah, Zedekiah, is overthrown and killed—when, in seeming conflict with Jacob, *the scepter departs*[9]—it is a shattering blow to those who have held fast to God's promise that he will establish through David a royal throne forever.

Judah is where Jerusalem is located, home of the Temple and the Ark of the Covenant. The Ark has been the very presence of God among his people since the time of Moses. When Nebuchadnezzar conquers Judah, he destroys the Temple and the Ark vanishes into the mists of history.[10] For the Judahites in Babylon, it is not only a geographic exile but a spiritual one.

Perhaps nothing so captures the sorrow and desolation of this time than Psalm 137, a Lament over the Destruction of Jerusalem. It is a cry of the heart from a Judahite captive in Babylon, taunted by his captors to sing a Psalm of joy and praise, *a song of Zion*, and unable to do so because of his sufferings:

> By the waters of Babylon,
> there we sat down and wept,
> when we remembered Zion....
> For there our captors
> required of us songs, saying,
> "Sing us one of the songs of Zion!
> How shall we sing the LORD's song
> in a foreign land?

The Babylonian Captivity ended in 539 BC when Babylon itself was conquered by the Persian king Cyrus the Great. Cyrus, like David before him, recognized Jerusalem's status as a holy city. Cyrus allowed the exiles to return to Judah and encouraged them to rebuild the Temple. With great effort, they did so, and musicians were able to "sing the songs of Zion" once again.

The Temple, however, no longer housed the Ark of the Covenant, lost during the Babylonian Captivity. And no son of David reigned.

David's line continued through the deposed prisoner-king Jeconiah. Jeconiah, however, had offended the Lord, and in consequence had been cursed. Jeconiah's offspring, said the Lord, would never sit on David's throne.[11] With Zedekiah's sons murdered and Jeconiah's cursed, the royal dynasty of David seemed at an end.

Judah continued to exist, no longer as a kingdom, but as a province of a foreign empire. With one brief interlude, that would be its fate through a succession of empires—Persian, Greek, Roman.

Glimmers of Hope

After the conquest of Nebuchadnezzar, Judah was ruled first by Persia, then later by Alexander the Great and the Hellenistic dynasties that succeeded him. Even as a foreign province, Judah recovered a degree of autonomy; its scepter had not departed completely. Judah's internal affairs were administered by Jewish governors and later, high priests. The first governor after the return from Babylon was Zerubbabel, a grandson of Jeconiah and thus a descendant of David.

For a brief period, Judah regained independence under the heroic Maccabees. As the Persian king Cyrus had done earlier, the Maccabees provided a partial fulfillment or prefiguring of the Messiah. They revived the lost kingdom. They rededicated the Temple—an action commemorated by the holiday Hanukkah—after the foreign tyrant Antiochus IV defiled it by setting up an altar to Zeus and sacrificing a pig within.

The Maccabees were great military leaders. The Messianic prophecy of David seemed to apply to them, at least in part: God made of their enemies a footstool, placing them under their feet.

They were not, however, of the line of David. Their kings would form the separate Hasmonean dynasty. And their reign would be tumultuous and short.

After the Babylonian conquest, God's promise to David that his kingdom is *firm forever* seemed impossible to believe. So many of God's people were scattered to the empires of their conquerors.

The house of David as a political entity was degraded; after a time, it effectively ceased to exist.

Still, the prophets keep hope in God's promise alive.

God *will* gather his people. He will send them a true servant of the Lord, who *will* listen to him, as David had done.

God *will* redeem his people, without money[12] by himself providing the sacrifice,[13] as Abraham had prophesied long ago. His Messiah, his anointed one, will make firm the Temple sacrifice forever so that God may dwell with his people once again.

Before the Assyrian and Babylonian conquests, the prophets of Israel and Judah warned the people continually of the destruction they faced if they did not return to the Lord and forsake idolatry, adultery, covetousness, and neglect of the poor.

After the conquests, when the destruction had come to pass, the tone of the prophets changes. They remind Israel of God's covenant with David and offer words of hope.

Jeremiah was a prophet who personally experienced the destruction of Jerusalem by Nebuchadnezzar and afterwards fled to Egypt as a refugee. He warned Judah repeatedly of its coming destruction for its faithlessness. Our word *jeremiad* comes from his warnings and reproaches.

At the same time, Jeremiah offers very comforting assurance that God will, after the destruction, regather his scattered flock. He speaks to the Judahites this word from the Lord.

> I myself will gather the remnant of
> my flock from all the lands to
> which I have banished them and
> bring them back to their folds.[14]

Jeremiah explicitly promises that God's flock will be placed under a descendant of David. As an advisor to Zedekiah, Jeremiah had personally seen the last king of Judah captured and blinded, and his sons slain before him. He sees David's line *snapped*. But his prophecy from the Lord is firm and clear:

> I will raise up a righteous branch for
> David; As king he shall reign
> and govern wisely, he shall do
> what is just and right in the
> land.[15]

Jeremiah will later repeat the prophecy of the coming *righteous branch* or *just shoot* of David. And he will add something to it. Not only will the just shoot reestablish David's throne forever; during his reign, priests will never be lacking to make sacrifice before the Lord.[16]

Jeremiah is not the only prophet to speak of God gathering his people around a son of David. It is a theme for many of the prophets: Hosea[17] and Zechariah,[18] Ezekiel[19] and Isaiah.[20]

Ezekiel is a contemporary of Jeremiah. He is sent to Babylon about a decade before Jerusalem is destroyed by Nebuchadnezzar. He is a prophet-in-exile.

All around him, God's people have been scattered. But Ezekiel proclaims that God will regather his people. In Ezekiel chapter 37, God says he will reunite Judah and Israel; he will gather the Israelites from among the nations; he will even assemble the dead from their graves and put his spirit in them so that their dry bones may come to life!

Though the Temple is destroyed and the Ark has vanished, God will at that time dwell with his people once more:

> My dwelling shall be with them; I
> will be their God, and they will
> be my people.*[21]*

And though the line of David is ruptured, for Ezekiel, too, this rupturing is not the last world. *I will humble David's line*, the Lord had said, *but not forever*.[22] Zedekiah has been enslaved, his heirs murdered, his predecessor Jeconiah cursed. Nonetheless God reiterates through Ezekiel his ancient promise that in the reconstituted Israel, it will be his servant David who will rule:

> David my servant shall be king over them; they shall all have one shepherd.[23]

The Servant of the Lord

No prophet gives a fuller picture of this coming "servant of the Lord" than Isaiah, prophesying during the earlier Assyrian destruction of the kingdom of Israel.

Isaiah prophesies that he will be formed by God from the womb[24] and that through him, God will show his glory.[25] He will gather the descendants of Jacob, the twelve tribes, to himself. He will do even more: his mission will extend beyond the twelve tribes to the nations, or Gentiles. As had happened for a time with Solomon, the whole world will turn to this servant of the Lord for wisdom.

> It is too little ... for you to be my

> servant, to raise up the tribes of Jacob, and restore the survivors of Israel; I will make you a light to the nations, that my salvation may reach to the ends of the earth.[26]

Isaiah's servant of the Lord will be greater even than David. Yet paradoxically, his greatness is shown not in might and wealth and power but in meekness and humility. *A bruised reed he will not break*, Isaiah tells us, *and a dimly burning wick he will not quench*.[27] The servant of the Lord brings together two prophetic strands: the mighty king who will rescue his people from their enemies and the humble savior who will tend their wounds.

Other prophets, too, bring these strands together. The evangelists Matthew and John both point to an astounding prophecy of Zechariah in recounting Jesus' entry into Jerusalem on Palm Sunday: *Behold your king is coming to you, a just savior is he; humble, and riding on a donkey, on a colt, the foal of a donkey.*[28] But no one paints a more vivid picture of the coming servant king than Isaiah. This king will finally break the dynamic of which God had warned the Israelites. He will not exploit his subjects, but serve them—no matter the cost to himself.

> Here is my servant whom I uphold,
> my chosen one with whom I am pleased.
> Upon him I have put my spirit;
> he shall bring forth justice to the nations.
>
> I formed you, and set you
> as a covenant for the people,
> a light for the nations,
> To open the eyes of the blind,
> to bring out prisoners from confinement,
> and from the dungeon, those who live in darkness.[29]

WHEN THE ISRAELITES first approached the prophet Samuel to demand a king, God solemnly warned them: *You will become his slaves.*[30] One thousand years later, the Israelites had drunk this bitter truth to the dregs.

After a brief period of national glory under David and Solomon, Rehoboam pressed upon them a heavy yoke, shattering the nation into two kingdoms, Israel and Judah. It was the first of several shatterings to come.

Weakened by separation, and losing through idolatry the protection God had given them as his "people set apart," the two kingdoms were conquered and the people enslaved. The ten northern tribes were led captive to Assyria, disappearing from history. Judah was led to the waters of Babylon, there to mourn its fate.

Yet the prophets who had warned Israel of the consequences of disobeying God also offered hope. God's promise to establish David's throne forever remained in effect.

The last king of Judah, Zedekiah, had been deposed, and his sons slain. Still, a son of David and true servant of the Lord would one day rise. He would conquer his enemies, gather the scattered tribes, make Israel a light to the nations, and establish an everlasting sacrifice.

He would be the greatest of Israel's kings, its Messiah. And the Messiah, God's anointed, would set his people free.

4

TRIAL

ARE YOU THE KING?

Inside the house of Caiaphas, the high priest, the Jewish ruling council was trying Jesus of Nazareth on the charges of blasphemy.

Outside, Jesus' disciple Simon Peter watched silently and waited.

Three years ago, he had left everything when his brother Andrew came to him with astounding news: *We have found the Messiah!*[1]

In working, traveling, and living with Jesus, Peter experienced firsthand the reasons for Andrew's claim. Peter would later make it himself, and even go beyond it, telling Jesus, *You are the Messiah, the Son of the living God.*

After this confession, Jesus changed Simon's name to Peter, proclaiming him the "Rock" on which Jesus would build his Church.[2]

Now, however, the Rock was crumbling. The Messiah he had followed was not in the house of Caiaphas to be crowned but to be charged with blasphemy and sedition. The penalty was death—and Peter was terrified.

This uncertainty about Jesus at the moment of crisis was not unique to Peter. Of Jesus' twelve hand-picked disciples, all would succumb except his best friend, John.

Even the great prophet John the Baptist, whose entire mission in life was to point to Jesus as Messiah, wavered at the last. When his ministry ends not in triumph but imprisonment, with his fate in the hands of Herod Antipas,[3] he sends a message to Jesus. *Are you the one who is to come*, John asks, *or should we look for another*?[4]

Throughout his ministry, Jesus gave all around him many reasons to affirm he was the promised son of David. Yet, as his trial progressed, he appeared less like the mighty warrior-king who had slain Goliath and more like the last king of Judah, Zedekiah, who had tried to free his people but had been brought before a ruthless foreign conqueror to be tortured and destroyed.

∽

WHAT CONVINCED PETER, Andrew, and so many others Jesus was the Messiah?

Jesus was not a king in any obvious sense. True, he was a son of David—*descended from David,* as St. Paul would write, *according to the flesh.*[5] Matthew and Luke carefully document Jesus' royal pedigree. They record his birth in Bethlehem, the very town where David was born, and from which the Messiah was prophesied to come. *From you shall come forth for me one who is to be ruler in Israel*, God had said through the prophet Micah; *Whose origin is from of old, from ancient times.*[6] Jesus' mother and earthly father, Joseph, were not from Bethlehem, but in the Providence of God, they had been ordered to travel there late in Mary's pregnancy. Rome, which increasingly held the scepter in Judah, had decreed a census, ordering its subjects back to their patrimonial lands so they might be taxed.

For those with eyes to see, signs that Jesus was to be *ruler in Israel* were present at his birth. And the genealogies of Matthew and Luke are fascinating documents, showing, through Jesus' line of descent, God's faithfulness to his promises over many generations.

The genealogies, however, were written and compiled after Jesus' ministry by followers convinced he was the Messiah on other grounds.

For most of his earthly life, Jesus' Davidic descent, which he shared with others, wouldn't have been well-known—or, if it were known, given him much status. More relevant to Jesus' social standing was that he was putatively a humble carpenter's son and that he grew up in Nazareth, a town of such low regard that even one of Jesus' apostles, Nathanael, asked if anything good could come from there.[7]

David had been born over a thousand years earlier. The Davidic dynasty was long-ended, and new ones had arisen: the Hasmonean and, now, the Herodian. Not only was the house of David dethroned and socially degraded; the surviving royal line of David was, as we have discussed, seemingly subject to the *curse of Jeconiah*. The deposed king Jeconiah had survived Zedekiah and his heirs but been told by God, *None of your offspring will be king*.[8] The people of Judah longed for the promised son of David yet were baffled as to how he might appear.

A Voice from Heaven

Peter and the other apostles came to believe that Jesus was the Messiah, God's anointed, primarily because of the great miracles he worked during his public ministry.

Jesus' signs and miracles are attested by many ancient sources, biblical and nonbiblical alike. Even early *opponents* of Jesus and the Church acknowledged his miracles, often attributing it to sorcery—the kind once wielded, for example, by Pharaoh's magicians—rather than the power of God.[9]

Though Jesus' identity and destiny is revealed to a few at his nativity and during his infancy and childhood, he largely evades public notice for thirty years. Like his forefather David, Jesus spends most of his early years in obscurity. That changes when God discloses something of his mission through an encounter with a prophet.

David's encounter was with Samuel in the fields of Bethlehem. Jesus' encounter is with John the Baptist, the last prophet of the Old Covenant, on the banks of the Jordan River. It is here at his baptism that he is revealed publicly as the Messiah when the Spirit of the Lord descends upon him visibly[10] in the form of a dove.

By definition, the Messiah is an *anointed* king; he's chosen and consecrated for his role by God, just as David had been. He doesn't simply inherit his throne—or worse, seize it, as many of the kings of Israel had. No, he is chosen by God, *a king that God will choose,*[11] as Moses had said. This is confirmed through a prophet's, and later a high priest's, anointing.

Unlike any other biblical figure described or portrayed as anointed, Jesus was filled with the Holy Spirit from the very instant of his being.[12]

Saul was anointed king of Israel as an adult. David received his first anointing as a boy. John the Baptist, the "greatest of the prophets,"[13] was filled with the Holy Spirit as a child still in the womb.[14]

But only Jesus is *conceived* by the Holy Spirit. John will later say in his Gospel that God gives Jesus his Spirit *without measure*.[15] At the baptism of Jesus, God reveals publicly what has always been the case: Jesus is filled with the Holy Spirit.

The visible descent of the Holy Spirit upon Jesus is a *theophany*, recalling earlier theophanies to Moses and the Israelites at Mount Sinai. It signals God is preparing to intervene in history in an extraordinary way. The dove reminds us of the dove Noah released from the ark. It points to the new creation Jesus is inaugurating: the kingdom of God.

The descent of the Spirit is not the only extraordinary manifestation at the baptism of Jesus. A voice from heaven also booms out to the crowd:

> You are my beloved Son; with you I
> am well pleased.[16]

The heavenly words are rich with meaning. They point back to both Isaiah's servant of the Lord prophecy and God's promise to David.

The voice declaring Jesus "my beloved Son" recalls the Dynastic Oracle, God's promise that the Messiah will be a descendant of David and *a son to me*.[17]

And the phrase *with you I am well-pleased* alludes to Isaiah's "servant of the Lord" prophecy: *Here is my servant whom I uphold, my chosen one with whom I am pleased.*[18]

Here again we have the prophetic strands announcing a son of David and a servant of the Lord fused into one. At his baptism, God declares to all present that Jesus is both, addressing the assembly of the people even more directly and intimately than he had at Sinai.

It is after this that Andrew finds Peter and tells him: *We have found the Messiah.*

The Call of the Twelve

After his baptism, Jesus begins his public ministry. He chooses twelve men, Peter and rest of the apostles, to accompany and assist him. The establishing of the Twelve is a Messianic act, a symbolic regathering of the tribes of Israel. It is another reason why Jesus stirred such hopes that he was the Messiah.

Jesus' decision to select the Twelve as his special collaborators is crucial. He tells them that in the age to come, when he is enthroned as king, they too will have thrones and judge or govern the twelve tribes of Israel.[19]

Recall that at the time of Jesus, the twelve tribes have largely disappeared from history. It has been a thousand years since they were united under David and Solomon; since then, they have been split, scattered, and exiled.

It is now largely the descendants of just one tribe who are "set apart" and trying to keep the Law of Moses in its fullness. That one tribe is Judah, from which the word *Jew* is derived.

In appointing the Twelve, Jesus' contemporaries would have understood him to be proclaiming the re-establishment of the Davidic kingdom, a time when the twelve tribes were united and Israel was a power on the world stage.

It must have been tremendously exciting. So many of the prophets, writing in the aftermath of the Assyrian and Babylonian exiles, had spoken of a son of David who would rule Israel and gather back the scattered tribes. Could that long-promised time have finally arrived?

A partial fulfillment of the prophecies of a regathering of God's people and restoration of Israel had occurred after the Babylonian exile when the Persian king Cyrus decreed the Jews could return to their homes and rebuild the Temple.

But five hundred years later, after that return from exile, any hopes raised by Cyrus had been dashed.

The Jews were now under the heavy yoke of Rome. Most of the descendants of the twelve tribes were still scattered among the nations. Jesus' appointment of the Twelve was a statement that he would fulfill what Cyrus had not: the re-establishment, and reuniting, of David's kingdom.

A New Kingdom

At his trial, Jesus asserted his kingdom *is not of this world*.[20] It could coexist with Caesar; it had no ambitions to administer the details of civic life.

Yet if Jesus' kingdom is not "of" the world, from the very beginning, it was "in" it, in visible, powerful ways. He acted and spoke in the manner of a king, as one with unquestioned authority. This is yet another reason why Peter and the others followed him as Messiah.

People sometimes say that while Jesus was a great moral teacher or rabbi, he never claimed to be the Messiah. This view cannot survive an informed reading of the Gospels. It misses the significance of acts such as Jesus forgiving sins—a display not merely of royal but *divine* sovereignty—and issuing laws and amending them, as with his teachings on divorce and the force of the ritual requirements of the Law. It ignores what the Gospels affirm of Jesus repeatedly: *he spoke with authority.*[21]

The Gospels very meticulously record how the events of Jesus' life and his own actions reveal him to be the promised son of David. First, John baptizes Jesus and the Holy Spirit rests visibly on him—an event similar to, but even more striking than, Samuel's anointing of David. Then Jesus symbolically unites the tribes of Israel, as David had done, by appointing the Twelve.

Jesus calls himself a shepherd, the good shepherd, as David had been, and promises to gather his scattered sheep. [22]

Like David, Jesus is zealous for the house of the Lord[23] and for national worship. David had given his people the Psalms, and Jesus gives them the *Our Father*—like the Psalms, a prayer to be said regularly, daily, and one which expressly calls for the realization of God's kingdom: *Thy kingdom come.*

The Finger of God

In his regal bearing and authority, Jesus reminded those around him of Israel's greatest leaders, men like Moses and David. But his authority went well beyond theirs. At times, he performs actions that are unprecedented for any man; actions that previously in history had been reserved to the Lord God alone.

One example is subtle and easy to overlook. We have seen how God punished David for his census. When they conducted a census apart from the Law, kings and emperors in effect claimed for themselves the people God had set apart, disregarding *the ransom paid for their lives.* [24] Yet Jesus' knowledge of his followers is far more extensive than David's. He has enrolled each in a book of life.[25] He has counted not just their persons and belongings but *every hair on their head.*[26] His intimate knowledge of his people, achieved without the consequences triggered by David, points to the special status of Jesus—and hints, perhaps, at the ransom he will pay for their lives.

Another way Jesus' unique status is shown, far

more visibly and dramatically, is in his casting out of demons. Jesus exorcisms are a fulfillment of Isaiah's prophecy about the servant of the Lord, who *brings out prisoners from confinement, and from the dungeon, those who live in darkness.*[27]

In his exorcisms, Jesus sets himself apart from his Old Testament precursors and types. For all his kingly power, David never cast out demons. Nor did Moses. The only one we see before Jesus with authority over demons is the Lord himself, who cast down the so-called "gods of Egypt" and executed judgement against them.

The exorcisms of Jesus are signs that he is not simply the Son of David but the Son of God—not merely human, but also divine. There are others as well.

We have already mentioned his forgiving of sins, a divine prerogative. Jesus' opponents recognized the implicit claim to divinity. When Jesus tells the paralytic, *Friend, your sins are forgiven*, the Pharisees are thunderstruck. *Who is this fellow who speaks blasphemy?* They think to themselves. *Who can forgive sins but God alone?*[28]

Another sign of Jesus' divinity is his control over nature and the elements. At the Sea of Galilee, Jesus shows that even the winds and the waves obey him, just as they had obeyed the Lord when he parted the Red Sea for the Israelites.

Jesus not only *controls* nature; he also *creates*. He creates wine from water at Cana.[29] He creates bread and fish openly in front of multitudes, feeding them miraculously,[30] as the Lord had fed their ancestors in the wilderness with manna from heaven.

He creates life itself. He comes before the corpses of the daughter of Jairus,[31] the son of the widow of Nain,[32] and his friend Lazarus,[33] three days in the tomb. They are all dead, their bodies starting their return to the *dust of the earth*[34] from which all men come. Yet his word summons forth what is no longer there. He calls all three from death to life.

At every moment in his public ministry, Jesus' kingly authority as the Son of David radiates forth. But there are certain moments when Jesus works a sign so astounding—casting out demons, commanding the waves, *creating* bread and fish, calling the dead to life—that he reveals a mystery greater still. His actions invite the crowds to exclaim, as Pharaoh's magicians who witnessed the judgement of Egypt did long ago, *Here is the finger of God.*[35]

Good News to the Poor

Jesus had reminded the crowds of David's prophecy about the Messiah in Psalm 110 that God would make his enemies his footstool and place them under his feet.[36] In his signs and miracles, in his driving out of the demons which assailed his people, Jesus displayed the power of the Messiah.

Jesus also showed another attribute not often associated with conquering kings. He was able to read the hearts of each person he encountered[37] and give them his personal and tender love.

The poet E. E. Cummings gives us words to describe the tenderness of Jesus to the poor, the outcast, and the shunned: *vainly no smallest voice might cry / for he could feel the mountains grow.*[38] The prophet Isaiah says of him something similar: *A bruised reed he will not break and a dimly burning wick he will not quench.*[39] Matthew applies these very words to Jesus, showing he is the one foretold by Isaiah, the servant of the Lord.

Early in his public ministry, Jesus returns to his hometown of Nazareth and preaches in the synagogue there. He begins by reading from a passage of Isaiah concerning the servant of the Lord:

> The Spirit of the Lord is upon me,
> because he has anointed me

>to bring glad tidings to the poor.
>He has sent me to proclaim liberty
>>to captives
>and recovery of sight to the blind,
>to let the oppressed go free,
>and to proclaim a year acceptable to
>the Lord.[40]

All eyes are on Jesus as he reads this passage from a scroll. He concludes by saying, *Today this scripture passage is fulfilled in your hearing.*

Jesus is very clearly saying he is Isaiah's servant of the Lord. And he is inaugurating his ministry with a kind of Jubilee of Mercy. He will reach out to adulterers, tax collectors, lepers, Samaritans—all those who in one way or another have been spiritually exiled from the community—and bring them home.

In establishing his kingdom, Jesus will change a dynamic that had burdened the Israelites almost from the time they first had a human ruler. God had warned, when the Israelites had asked for a king, *you will become his slaves.*[41] But now, in Jesus' kingdom, the leader would become the servant of all. When Jesus saw the Twelve squabbling about who was chief among them, he took them aside and said:

> You know that the rulers of the Gentiles lord it over them, and the great ones make their authority over them felt. But it shall not be so among you. Rather, whoever wishes to be great among you shall be your servant; whoever wishes to be first among you shall be your slave.[42]

This shift to servant leadership is the first of many changes. Another follows quickly, as king Jesus will not limit his care to the descendants of Jacob, to the "people set apart." While his ministry begins with the Jewish people, it extends beyond them, taking in Samaritans, Canaanites, even the hated Romans. The way in which Jesus draws these foreigners to himself is yet another reason why Peter and the apostles believed, and the crowds hoped, that he was the Messiah.

Both Mark and Matthew tell us of a Canaanite or Syro-Phoenician woman who comes to Jesus asking him to free her daughter from a demon.[43] She is a Gentile coming to the Son of David to ask a favor, and Jesus, at first, rather shockingly puts her off: *It is not right to take the food of the children,* meaning Jews, he says, *and throw it to the dogs*, meaning Gentiles.

Yet the woman persists, and we should imagine Jesus is affectionately inviting her to do so. *Even the dogs eat the scraps that fall from the table of their masters*, she responds.

The language of dogs and children is a little jarring. But what the woman is saying is essentially what Isaiah said of the servant of the Lord: *It is too little for you to raise up the tribes of Jacob; I will make you a light to the nations, that my salvation may reach to the ends of the earth*. In other words, Jesus prompts the Syro-Phoenician woman to profess that he is the Messiah, and as Messiah, his mission is not only to Israel but to the world.

Another great profession of faith in Jesus comes from a centurion in the town of Capernaum, with a servant who is ill.[44] Like the Syro-Phoenecian woman, the centurion is a Gentile; in fact, he's a *Roman*, commanding one hundred of the soldiers subjugating Judea.

The centurion is a man of authority, yet he entrusts his servant completely to Jesus. He humbly confesses that he is not worthy for Jesus to enter under his roof—a confession repeated at every Mass—and proposes instead that Jesus only say the word and his servant will be healed. It is a striking example of faith by the centurion.

And it is a confirmation, by a soldier of the mighty Roman Empire, of the even greater might of the Messiah.

Heaven's Silence

Peter and the other apostles had many compelling reasons to give up everything to follow Jesus as Messiah.

They knew of his anointing with God's spirit. They had been promised positions of authority in his kingdom, ruling over the twelve tribes.

Peter witnessed Jesus act with an authority greater than Moses and David, as he cast out demons, commanded nature, raised the dead, and proclaimed the law of his kingdom.

Peter had seen Jesus gather outcasts, exiles, and Gentiles to himself. And he had watched a Roman centurion come to Jesus and place himself at his feet.

Memories of some or all these events surely raced through Peter's mind as he waited outside the house of Caiaphas.

But as the hours passed with Jesus in captivity —as more and more witnesses arrived to testify against him, as the fate that awaited him inched closer—Peter's happy memories would have begun to dissipate, driven out by a rising fear of what was to come.

The arrest of Jesus, his trial and then his Passion, are a complete reversal of his public ministry. During his ministry, even his enemies had been astounded by the authority with which Jesus taught and acted. But with his arrest and then trial, that authority appeared to evaporate.

Jesus did not resist when the Sanhedrin took him into custody; nor did his followers defend him.

And when Jesus is brought before Pilate, it is a very different experience than with the centurion from Capernaum. Now Rome in all its might is unbowed.

We have seen that the Old Testament is in part a chronicle of God's interventions to answer the taunts of his enemies.

Pharaoh taunts Moses, *"Who is the LORD, that I should obey him?* and God answers spectacularly with the ten plagues and the parting of the Red Sea. Goliath jeers at Saul and the Israelites, and God answers with David, who miraculously slays the giant with a single stone. The Assyrian king Sennacharib boasts he will destroy Jerusalem; he is forced to retreat as 185,000 of his soldiers are slain in the middle of the night.

When Jesus is put on trial for his life, those who believed or hoped he was the Messiah had good reason to expect another miraculous intervention. But as the day wears on, as the jeers increase, as Jesus is struck and mocked—as he is dragged closer to the scourging, the forced march up Cavalry, the excruciating crucifixion—there is no miracle, no spectacular response from heaven, no divine rescue or display of power. Heaven is silent.

During the trial of Jesus, even before the sentence of death is given, Pilate orders Jesus scourged. Scourging as practiced by the Romans was pure agony. It was also debasing and humiliating, and this was Pilate's intent. Scourging was so inhumane that it was forbidden to Roman citizens; the victim was stripped, bound to a post, and eviscerated with weighted and hooked whips that literally tore open his back to the bone.

The scourging of Jesus was meant to humiliate him, disfigure him, and erase from the mind of the crowd any thought or hope he was the Messiah who would restore the throne of David. Every lash was a taunt: *Behold your king!*

PETER'S TIME in the courtyard ended with his famous three denials predicted by Jesus himself.

Peter had staked his life on the reality that Jesus was God's anointed one. He had seen Jesus' miracles and mighty works. He had seen his kingdom take shape before him and had been promised the position of "Rock" within it; he had seen Jew and Gentile alike come to the feet of Jesus and declare him Messiah and Lord.

Peter had made this declaration himself. Yet in Caiaphas' courtyard, he had withdrawn it, repudiating Jesus as his power seemed to collapse and he moved closer to being handed over to Rome.

We can only speculate as to all Peter felt in the courtyard. He and the apostles had been prepared by Jesus, told in advance that as Messiah, he would have to suffer and die. Just hours before, Jesus had anticipated his Passion at the Last Supper and presented it not as a defeat at the hands of men but as a self-offering to the Father for the sake of the whole world.

But in the darkness, with Jesus' harsh interrogation proceeding inside, and torture looming at the hands of Rome, Peter faltered, as did his fellow apostles. Among the Twelve, only John would accompany Jesus through the day ahead.

John took his place at the foot of the Cross, beside Mary, Mother of Jesus. They held fast to the promises they had been given and trusted, even in the very valley of the shadow of death.

5

ASCENSION

AT THE RIGHT HAND OF GOD

What Peter feared in the courtyard of Caiaphas' house had come to pass.

Jesus had been tried, mocked, and sentenced to death, and none had come to his aid. He had been scourged, crowned with thorns, then presented to the crowd—a cruel taunt to those who hoped he would be king.

Jesus carried a cross up the hill of Calvary, was nailed to its beams, and died. He marched through the Valley of the Shadow of Death, and at the peak of darkness, he was not rescued but cried out, *Eli, Eli, lema sabachthani?*[1] That is, *My God, my God, why have you forsaken me?*

Yet fifty-two days after his denials in the courtyard, on the feast of Pentecost, Peter openly proclaimed this Jesus who had been crucified was indeed Messiah and Lord.

Many witnessed Jesus' humiliation and death. Yet Peter witnessed something else, and this time, he would not remain silent.

Jesus *had* walked through the valley of the shadow of death. He walked all the way through. He was not spared death, as others had been, but had instead confronted it in battle and prevailed. The execution meant to prevent his kingdom had in fact initiated it. It had unleashed an anointing so powerful that after it, all was changed, changed utterly: the kingdom of God was born.

WHAT GAVE Peter his unshakeable faith that Jesus, crucified atop Mount Cavalry just outside Jerusalem's walls, was indeed the Messiah? We know the answer, of course: the Resurrection.

The risen Jesus appeared to Peter and all the apostles, and to many others as well.[2] The same Jesus Peter traveled with, lived with, and ate with, ate with him again.

Jesus was so physically present that he could show his apostles the wounds from his Passion and invite "doubting Thomas" to probe. He was no ghost.

Yet he *was* different. Walls, locked doors, and space itself were no longer obstacles. He came and went at will. He veiled and revealed his identity as he chose. His kingship extended to the very fabric of creation. He was, as the Church proclaims him, *Lord of the Universe*.

Lord of the Universe

Old Testament prophets portray the Messiah as a strong king, a conqueror, none more so than David. The first verse of David's Psalm 110 is quoted many times in the Bible, by Peter,[3] Paul,[4] and, as we have seen, Jesus himself.[5] It is one of the key Messianic prophecies:

> The LORD says to my lord: "Sit at
> my right hand, while I make
> your enemies your footstool."

During his ministry, Jesus impressed all who encountered him with his authority, inspiring the hope that he was indeed the Messiah. At his trial, these hopes collapse. The Messiah is to be a conqueror like David; but here is Jesus, brought bound before a foreign occupier, not like David, but Zedekiah, the last, failed king of Judah.

Yet when Peter and the apostles encounter the

risen Christ, their hopes not only revive but they obtain an unshakeable conviction Jesus is indeed Lord and Messiah.

In the stirring words of the *Exsultet*, Jesus *broke the prison-bars of death and rose victorious from the underworld*. He proved himself a conqueror and placed his enemy under his feet.

To achieve this victory, he had first to die. He would vanquish his enemies not through sheer divine omnipotence but through his five most sacred wounds. He would allow himself to be struck so that, like the rock that had accompanied the Israelites during their wandering in the wilderness,[6] life-giving water, mixed with his precious blood, might flow from his side.[7]

His crucifixion had not been coerced or imposed upon him. He had had the power to stop his executioners and tormenters at any time. As he tells his disciples in the Garden of Gethsemane, he can call upon his Father for *more than twelve legions of angels*[8] at any moment.

You refuse to speak to me? said Pilate to Jesus at his trial. *Do you not know I have the power to free you or crucify you?*

You would have no power over me, Jesus responds, *were it not given to you from above*.[9] Jesus' life is not taken. He lays it down willingly, drinking from the cup the Father has prepared.[10]

Prince of this World

Before the Resurrection, the crowds and even the apostles thought the "enemy" Jesus was confronting[11] in establishing his kingdom was Rome and the Jewish leaders who accused him of blasphemy.

After the Resurrection, they see he was opposing a far mightier foe. It was sin, death, and ultimately the devil Jesus faced in his Passion. The devil, after all, was the first enemy of God's people, targeting the woman, Eve. It is in response to this attack that God gives the *Protoevangelium*, the first promise of a conqueror-to-come. Church fathers such as St. Justin Martyr and St. Irenaeus identify the protoevangelium as the first prophecy of the Messiah:

> I will put enmity between you and
>   the woman, and between your
>   offspring and hers; he will crush
>   your head, while you will strike
>   at his heel.[12]

The protoevangelium foretells not just that the Messiah will crush the serpent; the Messiah himself will be struck. It is a prophecy of the

Passion, the means God's Providence will choose to break the devil's reign.[13]

Jesus defeats the devil on the Cross. His first encounter with the devil, however, is three years earlier. It occurs at the start of his public ministry following his baptism by John the Baptist when Jesus is revealed publicly as the Messiah.

Jesus had gone into the desert to fast and pray. There the devil, Satan, came to him. Satan showed Jesus all the kingdoms of the world in a single instant. Then he said:

> I shall give to you all this power and
>   their glory; for it has been
>   handed over to me, and I may
>   give it to whomever I wish. All
>   this will be yours, if you worship
>   me.[14]

This account of Jesus' temptation is fascinating for many reasons. One is it shows all the kingdoms of the earth in the devil's grip. Salvation history until this point has been the story of God setting the Israelites apart, dwelling with them, and keeping them holy and the nations of the world enslaving them, attacking, scattering, and demanding ransom.

Now we get a peek behind the curtain at the

unseen entity who has been orchestrating it all along. It is a being Jesus chillingly refers to as *the prince of this world.*

When Jesus rebuffs him, the devil takes Jesus to the highest point of the Temple—that sacred site that throughout salvation history has inspired such zeal, and such rage.

There the devil tells Jesus to cast himself from the Temple heights—a diabolical parody of the Sacrifice Jesus will make three years later on the Cross.

The devil tempts Jesus to "put God to the test." He wants Jesus to manipulate God, as Israel's first king, Saul, had attempted, offering a sacrifice it was not his to give. He wants Jesus to assert his own will, to grasp for himself what belongs to God. This was the devil's primal and continuing act of rebellion. Now he wants Jesus to make it too.

Jesus resists the devil, and the devil *departed from him for a time.* At the end of his ministry, Jesus answers the devil in full. Rather than seizing anything, he offers himself entirely to the Father, holding nothing back, in the perfect act of worship, trust, and love.[15] As Paul will write to the Colossians, it is this act that *delivers us from the power of darkness* and *transfers us to the kingdom of the Son.*[16]

The Road to Emmaus

Through his death and Resurrection, Jesus "ransomed Israel" once and for all, not with money, but with his Precious Blood.[17] He drove the devil from power. Forty days after his Resurrection, he would ascend into heaven to take his seat at the right hand of God.

In the Bible, the number forty is often associated with a time of preparation before a new phase of salvation history. The renewed creation given to Noah and his family takes place after forty days and nights of rain; the Israelites arrive at the Promised Land after forty years in the wilderness; Moses receives the Ten Commandments, and Jesus begins his public ministry, after forty days of fasting in the desert.

The period between the Resurrection of Jesus and his Ascension is also forty days. During this time, Jesus communicates to the apostles the reality of his conquest of sin and death, he enlightens them about why he had to suffer and die, and he prepares them for the inauguration of his kingdom at Pentecost.

One of the most famous of Jesus' Resurrection appearances occurs on the afternoon of the first Easter. Two disciples are walking from Jerusalem to Emmaus, a village about seven miles distant.

They are discussing the Crucifixion and the empty tomb discovered that morning and wondering what it all means.

Suddenly, the risen Jesus draws close. He conceals his appearance and joins their conversation.[18]

What are you discussing as you walk along? he asks.

The things that happened to Jesus the Nazarene, answers one of the disciples, named Cleophas. *Our chief priests and rulers handed him over to a sentence of death and crucified him. But we were hoping he would be the one to redeem Israel.*

Jesus scolds them for being slow to believe all that the prophets spoke. *Was it not necessary that the Messiah should suffer these things and enter into his glory?*

Then, *beginning with Moses and all the prophets*, Jesus shows them how his death and Resurrection were God's plan, foretold in the Scriptures all along. It is the very first Christian Bible study. And it is led by Jesus himself.

God Himself Will Provide the Sacrifice

We can only speculate on the scriptural passages whose meanings Jesus unlocked on that road to Emmaus. Many passages prophesy or foreshadow his Passion and Resurrection; unpacking them all would take much longer than that journey of a few miles.

We know Jesus began *with Moses;* that is, with the Pentateuch or Torah, the first five books of the Bible, to which Mosaic authorship is traditionally ascribed. One of the most striking prophecies of the Passion is there, in Genesis 22, where God tells Abraham, *Take your son Isaac, your only one, whom you love* and sacrifice him.

This passage has puzzled many readers. How can a good God command such a thing? And how can Abraham so cheerfully obey? Child sacrifice in the Bible is commanded by the demon gods Baal and Moloch. Why is it asked here by the Lord?

To understand this passage, we must recall God's earlier promise. God had already told Abraham he would become father of a multitude through Isaac and that these descendants would be set apart by God and given the Promised Land.

Abraham has unwavering faith in God's promise of descendants through Isaac. He knows if he is faithful to God, somehow Isaac will be restored. The Letter to the Hebrews says that as Abraham prepared to sacrifice Isaac, he *reasoned that God was able to raise even from the dead.*[19]

Abraham and Isaac head to the place of sacrifice, a place chosen by God. It is a site we have discussed before: Mount Moriah, or Zion. It is the spot where Jacob dreamed of a ladder between heaven and earth, and which David claimed for his capital and home. It is where David, at the command of the Lord, offered sacrifice to atone for his sins and to beg God's mercy on his people.[20] It is where Solomon built his Temple.

Today Mount Moriah can still be visited in Old Jerusalem at the Temple Mount, very close to the site of the Crucifixion.

As they head to that place of destiny, Isaac asks his father where the sacrificial sheep is. Abraham replies, *God himself will provide the lamb for the sacrifice.*[21] Then they arrive. Abraham binds Isaac and unsheathes his knife.

At the last moment, God sends an angel to stop the sacrifice and praises Abraham for passing this test of faith. It is a test with enormous significance. The binding of Isaac anticipates what would happen in the fullness of time at or near that very spot.

God himself would indeed provide the sacrifice, his own beloved Son—and then raise him from the dead.

Hidden in the Psalms

Prefigurings like that of Isaac are found throughout the Old Testament. In his preaching at Pentecost, Peter refers to David as a prophet who *foresaw and spoke of the Resurrection of the Messiah.*[22] He points specifically to Psalm 16—a prayer Peter and the Church after him sees as an expression of Jesus' trust, even during the Passion, that God will raise him from the dead.

> I saw the Lord ever before me . . .
> my flesh, too, will dwell in hope,
> because you will not abandon my
> soul to the netherworld,
> nor will you suffer your holy one to
> see corruption.[23]

In this Psalm, as in others, David is writing not in his own voice but in the voice of his promised descendant, the Messiah.

The Psalm can't literally be applied to David. As Peter points out, David's flesh *has* seen corruption. His tomb is in Jerusalem.

But the words of the Psalm *are* literally true of Jesus. Even in the midst of his Passion, Jesus' flesh dwelt in hope. Jesus would experience death but not the corruption of death. He would descend to the netherworld but not be abandoned there. God would raise him up and place him at his right hand forever.

The Psalm that foretells Jesus' Passion and Resurrection in the most striking manner is Psalm 22. Its first words are the ones cried by Jesus as he hangs on the Cross: *Eli, Eli, lema sabachthani?*[24] *My God, my God, why have you forsaken me?*

The Roman soldiers and others who heard Jesus cry out in this way must have considered it an anguished cry of defeat. But later, the disciples would see its profound significance. Though Jesus *was* in anguish, he was not defeated; he was in fact praying Psalm 22, a prophecy of both the Passion and the Resurrection.

Psalm 22 begins by recalling how God has rescued the Israelites in times past when they have called out to him, as in the Exodus from Egypt. Yet this time, the Psalmist, though he trusts in God, has not escaped.

> But I am a worm, not a man,
> scorned by men, despised by the people.
> All who see me mock me;
> they curl their lips and jeer;
> they shake their heads at me:

> "He relied on the LORD—let him
>   deliver him;
> if he loves him, let him rescue
>   him."*25*

The psalmist cries out because of his thirst, his parched mouth and throat. He speaks of men who, like lions, rend and lacerate him. They roar against him as his life drains away.

> Dogs surround me;
> a pack of evildoers closes in on me.
> They have pierced my hands and
>   my feet
> I can count all my bones.*26*

It's an incredibly vivid image of the Passion composed by David a thousand years before it occurs. It even predicts an event that all four Gospels record: *for my clothing they cast lots.*

Yet Psalm 22, which begins as a lament, ends as a Psalm of praise. For all his misery, the psalmist concludes by asserting that he will *give praise in the great assembly*. He affirms that God *heard me when I cried out*.

Somehow, despite the psalmist's sufferings, even in and through them, God has revealed himself as king, the *ruler over the nations*. And his power will be remembered to the ends of the earth.

Pierced for Our Sins

The Psalms and the Pentateuch, Moses and David, both prophesy the sacrifice of Christ. So too do the prophets who follow them; among them, none more than Isaiah. Side by side with Isaiah's glorious prophecies of the Messiah, of his kingship and dominion, the sorrowful mysteries of his life are foretold.

We have already considered the mysterious figure of whom Isaiah speaks, the "servant of the Lord." This figure is also known to scholars by another name: "The Suffering Servant." The name comes from what Isaiah reveals in the last two of his four "servant songs."

In the first two songs, Isaiah tells us the servant of the Lord will fulfill all the traditional expectations for the Messiah. He will be the Lord's anointed, his chosen one; he will raise up the tribes of Jacob; he will be a light to the nations; princes will bow before him.

The third and fourth servant song, however, introduce a new element. The servant of the Lord will also be *a man of sorrows, acquainted with grief.*[27]

Like Jesus, the servant of the Lord will be scourged and mocked. He will not resist.

> I gave my back to those who beat me, my cheeks to those who tore out my beard; my face I did not hide from insults and spitting.[28]

The servant of the Lord anticipates the sufferings of Jesus to such an astonishing degree that the Church fathers referred to the Book of Isaiah as "the Fifth Gospel" or the "Gospel of the Old Testament."

As the great Bible translator St. Jerome remarks, Isaiah writes of the mysteries of Christ's life with such realism that "you would assume he was not prophesying about the future, but rather composing a history of past events."[29]

> But he was pierced for our sins, crushed for our iniquity. He bore the punishment that makes us whole, by his stripes we are healed.[30]

The weeks following the first Easter morning must have been an extended road to Emmaus experience for all the followers of Jesus. How their hearts burned as they read Moses and David and the prophets in the light of the Resurrection. Jesus had been present but veiled in the Scriptures from the beginning. Now the veil was torn; the meaning of the Scriptures laid bare.

The Virgin Will Conceive

The disciples' understanding of Jesus was deepened by their rereading of Scripture. Someone else was also helping them know Jesus more profoundly as Messiah. That someone was Mary, the Mother of Jesus, who was now in their midst.

Mary had been the very first person to profess Jesus Messiah. She did so before his birth, at the Annunciation, [31] when she believed and accepted the Archangel Gabriel's words: *You will conceive and bear a son ... the Lord God will give him the throne of his father David, and he will reign over Jacob's descendants forever.*

Mary's *fiat* (that is, "let it be done") to Gabriel at that moment brought about the fulfillment of another Messianic prophecy from Isaiah: *Therefore the Lord himself will give you a sign; the virgin will conceive and bear a son, and shall call his name Emmanuel.*[32]

Like other prophecies of the Messiah, the prophecy of the Virgin Birth becomes clear over time. In the original Hebrew, it is only implicit that the young woman, or *almah*, is a virgin; it becomes explicit when the Greek translation, known as the Septuagint, renders *almah* as *parthenos*. Even then, it is likely the phrase *the virgin will conceive* was long understood to mean a virgin shall marry and conceive a child in the normal way.

That's why Mary, a virgin who has given herself as a *handmaid of the Lord*, who has promised to *know not man*, asks *how can this be?* when the angel Gabriel tells her she will conceive and bear a son.

After her encounter with Gabriel, Mary comes to understand the true meaning of Isaiah's words. She is the virgin who will bear a son—and she will conceive him not with a husband but virginally, when *the power of the Most High will overshadow you*.

The reality of the Virgin Birth unlocks the richer meaning not only of Isaiah's prophecy of the Messiah but others as well—such as God's promise through the prophet Nathan that the Messiah would be not only a son of David but *a son to me*.[33]

It even solves the problem of the curse of Jeconiah, by which God seems to end the Davidic dynasty. Through Joseph, Jesus is a legal *heir* of Jeconiah, with a true claim to David's throne, without being an *offspring* or descendant of Jeconiah, whom God has said will never be king.[34]

Anointed for Death

Mary was the first to contemplate the Mystery of the Messiah's birth. She was also the first to contemplate the Mystery of his Passion.[35]

Mary had been warned, if obliquely, of Jesus' Passion just forty days after his birth when she and Joseph presented Jesus in the Temple. There, a man named Simeon, filled with the Holy Spirit, took the child Jesus in his arms and praised him as God's salvation, his light to the nations, and the glory of Israel.

But Simeon also struck a more somber note. Jesus would also be *a sign that would be contradicted*. Then he turned to Mary and said, *a sword will pierce your soul too*.

In the days, months, and years that followed, Mary would recall Simeon's words often, pondering in her heart God's plan for her son.[36]

During Jesus' public ministry, the disciples are also given signs that he will suffer and die. One sign happens right at the baptism in the Jordan when Jesus is revealed as the Messiah, a prophet greater than John, and a king. Yet there is already a note of sacrifice: John the Baptist refers to Jesus as a Passover lamb, the *lamb of God who takes away the sins of the world*.[37]

The note of sacrifice deepens with Jesus'

anointing at Bethany. Jesus is dining with friends, including Lazarus, Martha, and Mary, and Mary of Bethany anoints Jesus' head and feet with expensive perfume. It is a lavish, extravagant gesture. Some of the disciples protest, yet Jesus praises Mary: *She is,* he says, *anointing my body for burial.*[38]

We have already seen how the concept of Messiah, the anointed king, had gone through successive waves of enrichment during the history of the Jewish people.

The roots go back to Moses. Moses tells the Israelites to avoid setting up royal dynasties like the pagans. They should pledge themselves only *to a king whom the LORD, your God, will choose.*[39] This is at the very core of what it means to be Messiah: *a king that God will choose.*

In the centuries that follow, layers of meaning are added to the word *Messiah*. At the height of the Davidic kingdom, we are told the Messiah will be a son of David who will conquer his enemies. He will be a light to the nations, like Solomon.

Later, the tragic experiences of scattering and exile add another dimension to *Messiah*. The Messiah will gather the lost tribes. He will heal the wounded and bruised. He will restore the Temple and ensure it is never destroyed or desecrated again.

Subtly intertwined with these meanings is

another. It is conveyed by Moses, David, and Isaiah. It is pondered by Mary in the silence of her heart. It is proclaimed at the baptism of Jesus when he is *anointed . . . with the Holy Spirit and power*.[40] And it is revealed at his second anointing at Bethany when he is prepared for burial.

Only, however, in the glorious light of the Resurrection does this meaning of Messiah become clear to the disciples. Only then do they understand God's plan for the Messiah to be more than a prophet, more even than a king. The Messiah is above all a priest, the high priest, who will offer the sacrifice of himself. He is the sacrifice that God himself will provide, the savior who allows himself to be struck, the one who will lay down his life for his friends.

FOR PETER AND THE APOSTLES, their forty days with the Risen Christ was a time of *looking back* —looking back at his words and actions during his public ministry, looking back at the mystery of his birth, looking back at Moses and David and the prophets and seeing them anew in the glorious light of the Resurrection.

The Resurrection appearances would end with the apostles *looking up*—at the Ascension. After teaching them why the Messiah had to suffer, and why their expectations had been incomplete, Jesus confirmed their desire for the Messiah's royal glory had not been mistaken.

The Ascension was Jesus' enthronement as Messiah and the inauguration of his kingdom;[41] he had driven forth *the prince of this world* and was now, definitively and everlastingly, *the king that God will choose*.

With his kingship would come a final anointing. His Baptism by John recalled Samuel's anointing of David. He had received a second anointing by Lazarus' sister Mary at Bethany. Nine days after his Ascension, a third and crowning anointing would come: the outpouring of the Holy Spirit at Pentecost.

This would be his anointing as king. It would be a superabundant anointing so powerful that it would overflow into his Mystical Body, the Church. It would impel the apostles, not to look *back*, or *up*, but *out*—to extend his kingship from Jerusalem and Judea, to the very ends of the earth.

6

PENTECOST
GO YE FORTH

The crowds who thronged round Peter near the Temple in Jerusalem saw a man boldly proclaim to thousands that Jesus was Lord and Messiah.

It was a miraculous transformation. Fifty-two days earlier, that same man had crouched in the shadows, fearing to make known his association with the Nazarene. Yet the transformation of Peter was not the miracle that drew the crowd.

The people pressed close around Peter that Sunday morning were a mixed group.[1] Some were residents of Jerusalem. Others were pilgrims, diaspora Jews from Europe, North Africa, Asia, and the Middle East. They had come to Jerusalem to observe the feast known in Hebrew as *Shavuot*.

Shavuot commemorates God's theophany on Sinai, the "day of the assembly" when God gave the Law, or Torah, and set Israel apart for himself.

This crowd had unexpectedly assembled around a house near the Temple. The house was the usual gathering place of the disciples. Today it was also the scene of some unusual phenomena. It was these phenomena that had drawn the crowd.

First, a noise like a rushing wind came upon the house. Then tongues of fire settled on each disciple inside. The flames were reminiscent of the fire that had descended upon Mount Sinai over 1,200 years before.[2]

Finally, all 120 disciples began to pray and praise God loudly. To the foreign pilgrims who were watching and listening, the prayers should have sounded like babble. Yet they did not. All those present, whether from Judea or abroad, heard the disciples praise God *in their own language.*

That was the miracle that drew the crowd to Peter. About three thousand of them would be baptized that day. And the Feast of Shavuot, better known as *Pentecost*, would forevermore commemorate an additional event: the establishment, or "birthday," of the Church.

WHAT HAD RUSHED upon the disciples at Pentecost and rested upon them like tongues of fire was, of course, the Holy Spirit.

The Holy Spirit had always been present in creation and in the history of God's people. The Nicene Creed calls the Holy Spirit the Lord, the giver of life. The Catechism tells us that he, together with the Son, is *the origin of the being and life of every creature.*[3]

In the Bible, the Holy Spirit, the Spirit of the Lord, is present right at the beginning of Genesis, *brooding over the waters.*[4] Throughout the Old Testament, he speaks through the prophets. The Holy Spirit rushed upon David after his anointing by Samuel,[5] a foretaste of the rushing at Pentecost.

Still, in Old Testament times, the Holy Spirit's presence had been mysterious, hidden, measured. On the Feast of Pentecost, that changed. The Holy Spirit arrived visibly and would forever after be present in the Church in fullness and in power.

At Pentecost, the Holy Spirit reveals himself; the mystery of the Holy Trinity is made known. More, the Spirit is *poured upon* the disciples of Jesus, poured upon his Mystical Body, the Church. In the Old Testament, the prophets and God's anointed ones had received a measure of the Holy Spirit. In Jesus, the Holy Spirit is present *without measure.*[6] At Pentecost, after the Ascension of the Messiah, that abundance, that overflowing of God's Spirit, is lavished on the disciples as well. It continues to be bestowed in the Church across the generations through the sacraments, particularly through the Sacrament of Confirmation.

The coming of the Spirit is linked directly to Christ's Ascension. *It is better for you that I go*, Jesus told the apostles at the Last Supper. *For if I do not go, the Advocate will not come.*[7] The outpouring of his Spirit followed his "going," his Ascension to his throne at the right hand of God. It was a final Messianic anointing, such as David had received on ascending the throne of Israel: his anointing as King. It overflowed onto his Mystical Body, the Church;[8] poured out with a lavishness and abundance prefigured in the earlier anointing at Bethany.

The Holy Spirit descends nine days after the Ascension. These nine days are a time of preparation. The apostles and other disciples gather with Mary, the mother of Jesus. They give themselves to prayer as they await the promised Advocate, the one who will remain and speak for the Lord.

The disciples' nine days of prayer gives rise to the devotion known as *novenas*. Today, Catholics and others seeking some special favor from God will often undertake a novena, nine days of special prayers. Novenas are a way of imitating Mary and the disciples as they prayerfully await the gift of the Spirit during the nine days between the Ascension and Pentecost.

The *time*, nine days, during which Mary and the disciples wait for the coming of the Holy Spirit is significant. The *place* where they wait is even more so. In the Bible, it is called simply the Upper Room.

The Upper Room

The Upper Room is, above all, the site of the Last Supper. It is known also as the *Cenacle*, from the Latin word for dining room. Since the fourth century, pilgrims have come to the Cenacle in the southern part of the Old City of Jerusalem, believing it to be the site where the Upper Room once stood.[9]

St. Epiphanius of Salamis, writing in AD 392, tells of a visit to Jerusalem by the Roman Emperor Hadrian in AD 117. Hadrian found "the whole city devastated," except for a few houses, seven synagogues, and one "church of God"; that is, one Christian church. The church, says Epiphanius, was built on Mount Zion at the site of the Upper Room.[10]

Today, the Cenacle is a site of religious significance to Jews, Muslims, and Christians. It is not currently a Christian shrine. But its importance to Christianity could not be greater. The Upper Room is quite simply the birthplace of the Church —a place set apart as the very first outpost of the kingdom of the Messiah.

Like other holy sites such as Mount Sinai, Bethlehem, and the nearby Temple Mount, the Upper Room is the location not just of one but of multiple great episodes in salvation history. It is astonishing to reflect on all the events in the life of the Church that happened in that one room.

The Upper Room is the scene of the Last Supper, the very first Mass. It is where Jesus establishes his priesthood, ordaining the apostles with the command *Do this in memory of me.*[11] It is where Jesus washes the feet of the apostles, demonstrating with this very intimate, humble gesture how they are to exercise leadership in his kingdom.[12]

The Upper Room is where Jesus gives his *Farewell Discourse*,[13] foretelling the coming of the Holy Spirit and the Church and revealing the inner life of the Holy Trinity. It is the most extraordinary revelation Jesus makes in the Gospels.

And in contrast with his sometimes cryptic way

of speaking to crowds during his public ministry—that is, through his use of parables and analogies—in the Upper Room, Jesus speaks plainly, clearly, directly. For the apostles, the Upper Room is a place of special intimacy with Jesus. It is the place where they transition from disciples to friends:

> I have called you friends, because I have made known to you everything I have heard from my Father.[14]

After the Crucifixion, the Upper Room becomes the disciples' gathering place. They come there for comfort and for refuge. They have good reason to be afraid of arrest, and worse, by the Sanhedrin.

While gathered in the Upper Room, the disciples have at least two powerful encounters with the risen Christ.[15] The first is the evening of Easter day. Though the doors to the Upper Room are locked, Jesus appears suddenly in their midst. He says, *Peace be with you,* and shows them his wounds. Then he sends them forth as his apostles, bestowing upon them his own divine power to absolve sins.

> Receive the Holy Spirit. Whose sins
>> you forgive are forgiven, and
>> whose sins you retain are
>> retained.

A week later, Jesus appears in the Upper Room again. He shows his wounds to "doubting Thomas," who had been absent during his Easter appearance.

That prompts Thomas to make history's first explicit, unqualified testimony to the divinity of Jesus:

> My Lord and my God!

Thomas' confession is followed, there in that first church of Christendom, by Jesus' famous blessing for everyone through the ages who has believed in his Resurrection and in his Real Presence.

> Do you believe because you have
>> seen me? Blessed are those who
>> have not seen and yet believe.

In the period between Holy Thursday and Pentecost, when the work of salvation is accomplished and the Church is born, it is the Upper Room that is the recurring assembly place of the disciples. The Upper Room is the new Tabernacle of the People of God. It is the place where the Lord is present, where he communicates his love, his life, and his will.

Throne Room of the King

In telling us about the Upper Room, the Gospels are uncharacteristically silent about exactly *whose* room it is. It was large, well furnished, and in a multistory building, so we know the owner—the "master of the house" as the Bible calls him—was wealthy.

Some have speculated the owner was Nicodemus or Joseph of Arimathea, wealthy Jewish leaders who were secret disciples of Jesus;[16] others that it was the family home of the evangelist St. Mark.[17] The Gospels don't say. Even the apostles don't seem to know. Peter and John meet the master of the house under odd circumstances after following signs given them by Jesus.[18]

The Gospels' preservation of the anonymity of the owner of the Upper Room suggests the evangelists wished to protect something. But what? Jesus had secret disciples during his ministry,

Nicodemus and Joseph of Arimathea, whom we have mentioned. Yet in due time, these secret disciples responded to the Lord's command to *confess me before men*.[19] The Gospel writers do not shy from proclaiming the names of Nicodemus and Joseph of Arimathea, to both men's everlasting glory.

It is possible the circumspection of the Gospels regarding the owner of the Upper Room is meant to protect not a person but a place; specifically, the resting place of Israel's most beloved king, David. We do not know for certain, but there is a tantalizing possibility that the Upper Room where Jesus inaugurated his kingdom was above King David's Tomb.

Modern day pilgrims to Jerusalem's Mount Zion discover the site of the Cenacle, or Upper Room, also memorializes the Tomb of David, directly below it.

Over the course of history, this spot has been a place of Jewish pilgrimage, Christian pilgrimage, and later home to a mosque as well. That is why the Cenacle, perhaps Christianity's holiest site after the Church of the Holy Sepulchre, is not today a major Christian shrine.

This is how the area is memorialized now, and has been for centuries. But does it reflect the historical reality? Is David now, or was he ever, truly buried here?

Did faithful Jews at the time of Jesus come to the Cenacle to venerate the relics of their long-dead king, pray for the arrival of the Messiah, and the restoration of David's throne?

This question is a matter of scholarly debate too complex to recount here.[20] Answering it requires not only archeological data but also a knowledge of how place names, such as Mount Zion, shift and expand over time; how Jerusalem's terrain has been reshaped by earthquake and construction and war; whether David's remains were ever reinterred, perhaps, for example, to protect them from invaders or grave robbers; and how to assess the reliability of both ancient written accounts and long-standing pious practices.

This is certain: the location of the Tomb of David was known at the time of Jesus. Peter implies he has visited it. He tells the Jerusalem crowds at Pentecost, *Brothers, I can tell you confidently that the patriarch David died and was buried, and his tomb is here to this day.*[21]

Peter does not reveal the location of David's Tomb. But where better than Mount Zion? Zion is the place of Abraham's sacrifice, David's palace, and Solomon's Temple. It is on Mount Zion where God, in the words of Psalm 2, *installs his king.*[22]

If Peter and other faithful Jews of his time visited the Tomb of David, they would have done so discreetly. They would have sought to avoid attracting the brutal notice of Rome and giving *what is holy to the dogs.*[23] They would have taken care as well not to arouse the jealously of Herod Antipas, or his avarice. A generation earlier, Herod's father, Herod the Great, had plundered David's Tomb.[24] Those who loved David and trusted in God's promises to him would not want that repeated. At the time of Jesus, it is reasonable to suppose the Tomb of David was maintained quietly, modestly, perhaps with the support of a few wealthy and devout Jews. Its location would not have been trumpeted.

From the outside, the Tomb of David might have appeared no more than a large two-story house, with an Upper Room above where trusted pilgrims were fed and lodged.

In the nearly two thousand years since Jesus' Last Supper, Jerusalem has been ravaged, rebuilt, transformed. The structure, appearance, and owner of the original Upper Room is a matter of conjecture; what was below it is unknown.

Still, it is fascinating to consider Jesus may have chosen for the birthplace of his Church and the throne room of his kingdom a spot directly over the resting place of his forefather, David—

who had been promised by God that his descendant would be the Messiah.

It would certainly be in character. As an infant, Jesus reveals his Messianic glory to his faithful servant Simeon.[25] During his ministry, he tells us Abraham *saw my day and was glad*.[26] On Mount Tabor, shortly before his Passion, he is transfigured before Moses and Elijah.[27]

It seems altogether fitting, and compatible with a careful reading of the Gospels, that Jesus would found his kingdom in the bodily presence of David, that "man after God's own heart," to whom the Lord had given his word so long ago:

> When your days have been completed and you rest with your ancestors, I will raise up your offspring after you, sprung from your loins, and I will establish his kingdom. He it is who shall build a house for my name, and I will establish his royal throne forever.[28]

Gathering the Tribes

Jesus himself specially chose the Upper Room for his Last Supper. After the Passion, the disciples return there. The Upper Room becomes their place of assembly, their *ekklesia*.

In the Septuagint, *ekklesia* refers to the Israelites assembled at Mount Sinai or for worship in the Temple. In the New Testament, *ekklesia* is no longer associated with a particular space but applies to any Eucharistic community. The *ekklesia* is wherever disciples of Jesus gather to *Do this in memory of me*.

The Christian assembly or *ekklesia* begins in the Upper Room, but it does not remain there. It will go forth to make new disciples, to gather the lost sheep, and to extend the kingdom of the Messiah.

At first, the assembly of the disciples is marked by timidity. The disciples gather in the Upper Room behind locked doors, fearful of arrest. That changes on the Feast of Pentecost. When the Spirit descends, the disciples pour forth from their gathering place, proclaiming *the mighty acts of God*.

The disciples receive the Holy Spirit and his seven gifts: *wisdom, understanding, counsel, fortitude, knowledge, piety, and fear of the Lord*. The names come from a prophecy in Isaiah about the qualities of the Messiah.[29] With their anointing by the Holy Spirit, the disciples now have a share in Jesus' messianic vocation. Jesus has inaugurated his kingdom, but they are to build it. They are to take up the messianic tasks announced by the prophets long before: to assemble the lost tribes, offer acceptable sacrifice, be a light to the nations, and place all enemies under their feet.

The first task is to assemble the tribes; in the words of the prophet Jeremiah, *to gather the remnant of God's flock and bring them back to their folds.*[30]

This was a task Jesus had symbolically initiated in several ways: by appointing the Twelve, by outreach to the Samaritans, descendants of the lost tribes, and by reconciling community outcasts. Though Jesus had begun the process, gathering the tribes of Israel remained largely a task for the Church.

In the first century AD, there were perhaps 500,000–700,000 Jews living in Judea and the surrounding regions. The worldwide Jewish population, however, was four to five million. Large Jewish communities thrived in Alexandria, in Syria, and throughout the Roman Empire. In fact, up to 10 percent of the empire was Jewish.[31]

These diaspora Jewish communities were a result of the Assyrian and Babylonian exiles, as well as later conquests of Judah. These conquests had seeded the empire and lands beyond it with Israelites and Jews who maintained the memory of God's promises and much of the Law but were separated from the Temple and longed for it. The Book of Tobit speaks movingly of an Israelite exile who pines for the Temple. It is a theme also in the Psalms.

> My soul yearns and pines
> for the courts of the LORD.
> My heart and flesh cry out
> for the living God.
> As the sparrow finds a home
> and the swallow a nest to settle her
>   young,
> My home is by your altars,
> LORD of hosts, my king and my
>   God![32]

Devout diaspora Jews who were able traveled periodically to Jerusalem to make sacrifice at the Temple. The pilgrimage to Jerusalem was a temporary salve to the wound of their dispersion. On Pentecost, however, the wound is healed in a radical way.

The whole experience of the first Pentecost in Jerusalem is a kind of reversal of the Tower of Babel. At Babel, in the generations after the Flood, God scattered humanity and introduced divisions into human language to prevent cooperation by corrupted peoples. He disrupted an attempted assembly of the nations rooted in human rebellion and pride.

At Pentecost, God does the opposite. He works a miracle so everyone hears the disciples speaking in their own native languages. The miracle marks the moment he is ready to unite his people—not in a man-made tower, but in the Church, the Mystical Body of Christ.

The Stumbling Block

The miracle at Pentecost gains Peter a hearing from the Jewish crowds. He converts many through his preaching, and perhaps even more through the miracles he and the apostles continue to work in the name of the Lord.

Many residents of Jerusalem, who had cried out *Crucify him!* at the trial of Jesus, are cut to the quick. As the prophet Zechariah had predicted, they looked upon the one they had pierced, and mourned.[33] Yet Peter offers hope. *Repent and be baptized for the forgiveness of your sins*, he tells them, *and you too will receive the gift of the Holy Spirit.*[34]

The Crucifixion, as St. Paul will later tell the Corinthians,[35] is the great "stumbling block" to Jewish acceptance of Jesus as Messiah. For the Jews, the idea of God allowing his anointed to undergo such extreme suffering and humiliation is almost impossible to reconcile with his might against Pharaoh, and Goliath, and Sennacherib, and so many of Israel's enemies from the past. Peter, the apostles, and first disciples have to help their fellow Jews climb over this stumbling block. They do so by making two points.

First, they demonstrate that the sufferings of the Messiah were part of God's plan, foretold by the prophets. As Peter preaches at Pentecost, Jesus was *delivered up by the set plan and foreknowledge of God*, who used *lawless men to crucify him*.[36] There was, after all, plenty of scriptural precedent for God using sin and apparent setback to bring about his plans. The rejection of the Lord's direct kingship at the time of the Judges had led to the establishing of the house of David and promise of a Messiah. The rebellion against Rehoboam had both preserved a faithful remnant and purified the desire for a regathering of Israel in God's appointed time. In Israel's very first generation, the betrayal of Joseph by his brothers led to his rising and power to save. Joseph's words to his brothers could be said all the more truly by Jesus: *You meant to harm me, but God meant it for good*.[37]

Second, in addition to demonstrating God's plan for the Passion, the apostles witness to the power of the Resurrection—a triumph and victory far greater than that of Moses and David. Moses had defeated Pharaoh, and David, Goliath. Only Jesus, however, had defeated death itself, as the apostles and more than five hundred others had personally witnessed.[38] The apostles' preaching brings a harvest of converts, at Pentecost and afterwards.

At Pentecost, the apostles and early disciples reach out to resident and visiting Jews in Jerusalem. In the years ahead, their reach will expand, radiating to the borders of the empire and beyond. They will bring the "lost sheep" back to God's fold. They will revive the "dry bones" of Israel, as the prophet Ezekiel had foreseen,[39] reassembling them within the restored kingdom of David, the Church.

An Acceptable Sacrifice

First generation disciples reach out to Jewish Christians and Jews in several inspired works. The Letter of James is addressed to the "twelve tribes in dispersion;"[40] the Letter to the Hebrews encourages Jewish Christians of the diaspora to hold fast to their faith; the Gospel of Matthew sets forth how Jesus of Nazareth is the one the Jewish prophets foretold.

The apostles reach out not only in writings but in their personal ministry. All except John will be martyred in foreign lands, where they will go to establish churches, *ekklesia*.

They assemble the scattered tribes in a manner the prophets likely never conceived; not by bringing back the diaspora Jews to Judea, but by bringing them *into* the Church.

During his public ministry, Jesus prepared the apostles for the time when he would replace the Temple sacrifice. He told the Samaritan woman that true worshipers would soon worship not at the Temple in Jerusalem but *in Spirit and truth*.[41] He told the Jews in Jerusalem, *Destroy this temple and in three days I will raise it up*.[42] He told the apostles at the Last Supper, in the Upper Room, *In my Father's house there are many dwelling places*.[43]

These statements must have seemed mysterious at the time. But after the Resurrection, they would become clear. Jesus was establishing a new covenant. Its Temple would not be a building in Jerusalem but his Mystical Body. Its assembly, its *ekklesia*, would take shape not only on one mountain or holy site but *wherever two or three are gathered together in my name*.[44] And its sacrifice would not be burnt offerings but his own flesh and blood, offered once and for all on Calvary and made present at every Holy Mass.

For devout Jews and Israelites, there was no greater joy than to be in God's Temple, and there was no greater sorrow than when the Temple was desecrated or destroyed. Safeguarding the Temple was one of the key prophetic promises related to the Messiah.

The Messiah, the prophets said, would establish a sanctuary forever,[45] where priests would never be lacking to make sacrifice.[46]

As regards the Temple in Jerusalem, this prophecy failed. The Temple was destroyed by the Babylonians, and its successor, the Second Temple, was destroyed by the Romans in AD 70. It has never been rebuilt.

But the apostles came to understand after the Resurrection that the true sanctuary could never be a building made of stone. The dwelling place of the Lord was the Church, his Mystical Body. And the Eucharistic offering, the Holy Mass, was the sacrifice that would never end. It would be available not only in Jerusalem but wherever the Lord's apostles and priests offered it *in persona Christi*, repeating his words from the Last Supper:

> Take this, all of you, and eat of it:
> for this is my body which will be
> > given up for you...
> Do this in memory of me.

In its very first generation, the Church goes

forth far from Jerusalem. In her members, the Lord is present in many communities over a vast area. By her growth, the Church achieves and lives the reality the poet Gerard Manly Hopkins will point to some eighteen centuries later:

> For Christ plays in ten thousand
>   places,
> Lovely in limbs, and lovely in eyes
>   not his
> To the Father through the features
>   of men's faces.[47]

PETER'S HARVEST on the first Pentecost was bountiful, gathering hundreds of Israel's scattered sheep. When they returned to their diaspora communities—in Alexandria and Antioch, Damascus and Rome—they surely missed the architectural splendor of Jerusalem's great Temple. But their absence from Jerusalem would not cause them to *pine for the courts of the Lord* or their *heart and flesh to cry out for the living God*. He would be with them in their own diaspora cities, dwelling with them through faith and baptism. And in a unique way, he would be present in the Holy Mass, the Messiah's sacrifice that would never end.

Within thirty years, James, leader of the Church in Jerusalem, will refer to *myriads* (that is, tens of thousands) of Jewish Christians in Judea and Palestine.[48] Many more are present among the diaspora.

By the end of the first century AD, the Church will have grown like the mustard seed to which Jesus had compared it. From the 120 disciples at Pentecost through the first harvest of 3,000 and the many that followed, the Church will have grown to perhaps one million faithful worldwide.[49]

Increasingly, the faithful were of Gentile origin, as the Church fulfilled its appointed task to be a light to the nations. But its first members would forever be drawn from Israel's scattered sheep. For them, the new *ekklesia* would always have a special meaning. The Church brought them into a restored kingdom of David; it was the Temple of God, present in their place of exile, offering the sacrifice that would never end. Reigning as king was the Messiah, the one promised to their ancestors. He had been crucified, yes, but was now risen, emerging victorious and glorious through the valley of the shadow of death.

The glory of Christ and his Church was compelling, and in the Apostolic age and afterwards, it attracted many. Christ had defeated sin and death in his Passion and toppled the devil from his throne; yet opposition, human and diabolical, remained. The Lord in his Mystical Body, the Church, would now press forward on two crucial Messianic tasks: becoming a light to the nations and putting all enemies under his feet.

7

PAUL

A LIGHT TO THE NATIONS

Around AD 35, just a few short years after the birth of the Church at Pentecost, a detachment of men set out from Jerusalem to the city of Damascus in Syria.

They were traveling to call upon the Jewish diaspora there and to find who among them had become "followers of the Way"; that is, believing and baptized Christians. The high priest in Jerusalem had given their leader, Saul, arrest warrants for any Jewish-Christians he found. Saul planned to bring them back in chains.

As the detachment approached Damascus, it was overpowered by a blinding light and booming voice that forced the men to the ground. Only Saul could hear the words.

> Saul, Saul, why are you persecuting
> me?

"Who, who are you, sir?" Paul managed respond.

> I am Jesus, whom you are
> persecuting. Now get up and go
> into the city and you will be told
> what you must do.[1]

The extraordinary encounter lasted just moments. When the light vanished and the men regained their feet, Saul was temporarily blinded. Nothing else seemed changed.

In fact, *everything* had changed—for Saul, the Church, for history itself.

Saul had set out on that road to Damascus as perhaps the most zealous enemy of the Messiah, Jesus. He had been thrown to the ground and placed like a footstool at his feet.

Yet, in conquering him, Jesus had raised him up. When Saul arose, he was no longer an enemy but an emissary. In the years to come, he would be known to the world by his Roman name, Paul— the great Apostle to the Gentiles, the man set apart and chosen by the Lord Jesus to bring his light to the nations.

THE MAN who became the Apostle Paul was born in Tarsus in modern day Turkey. Chief city of the Roman province of Cilicia, Tarsus was renowned for its culture and wealth.

Tarsus had been claimed in 333 BC by Alexander the Great. Later, it was ruled by Alexander's Greek successors for hundreds of years. Rome annexed the city in 67 BC.

Paul doesn't tell us how his family arrived in Tarsus. They were diaspora Jews, refugees uprooted by conquest and persecution. They thrived in their new home, even achieving Roman citizenship.[2] Yet they held fast to Jewish law and teaching. For the boy Saul, it was the very core of his life.

Zeal for the Law

The Apostle Paul is one of the most well-documented figures of ancient history. Of the twenty-seven books of the New Testament, thirteen are letters bearing his name. Another, *Acts of the Apostles*, recounts Paul's conversion, preaching, and missionary journeys.

Paul's most striking quality as a youth and

young man was his zeal for the Law of Moses. In his letters, Paul tells us he was one of the most devout and learned Jews of his generation,[3] circumcised on the eighth day, blameless in obeying the commandments.[4]

He tells us twice he's a member of the tribe of Benjamin[5]—the one tribe that remained with Judah and the line of David when the ten tribes broke away after Solomon's reign.

Paul is the only apostle the Bible identifies as a Pharisee, the strictest and most scholarly of the different Jewish groups at the time. In the Gospels, we often see Pharisees in conflict with Jesus, but there was much to admire about them.

The Pharisees believed in the blessing promised by the Psalms for those who delight in the Law, who meditate on it day and night.[6] They were vigilant about keeping the Law because they knew the disasters that befell Israel whenever the people abandoned the Law and adopted pagan ways.

Paul's family likely fled to Tarsus to escape persecution by a foreign conqueror. Around 167 BC, the Greek king Antiochus IV Epiphanes desecrated the Temple with an altar to Zeus, sparking an uprising and further dispersion of the Jews.

In 63 BC, there was another flight of refugees

when the Roman general Pompey besieged and conquered Jerusalem and strode into the Temple, desecrating it by entering the Holy of Holies, reserved to the high priest alone.

Jewish families like Paul's who experienced such sacrileges would have seen them as signs of divine displeasure—punishments from God for the people's failure to keep the Law.

As Saul studied the history of his people—first in Tarsus, later in Jerusalem under the famous scholar Gamaliel—one truth loomed large. God had set apart his people for a high destiny, but as he had warned Solomon long ago, that destiny required strict observance of his Law.

> If ever you turn away and forsake
> my commandments ... I will
> uproot the people from the land
> I gave and repudiate the house I
> have consecrated for my name.[7]

Upon reaching manhood, Saul dedicated his life to the Law and to opposing all who would rebel. It was this dedication that brought him into conflict with the newborn Church — and with a young man named Stephen, remarkably similar to himself.

Stephen's Testimony

Stephen is the first Christian martyr, the first disciple to bear witness to Christ at the cost of his life. We know from *Acts* that, like Paul, Stephen was a Hellenist—a Jewish-Christian, perhaps with roots in a diaspora community, heavily influenced by Greek culture and thought.

Stephen was like Paul in a number of ways. According to tradition, Stephen was also a student of the Rabbi Gamaliel. He had a deep knowledge of Jewish history and was a fearless and mesmerizing speaker.

Stephen was ordained a deacon to help care for the poor and widows. He was best known for his debates in the synagogues, where he would boldly proclaim Jesus as Messiah and show how Jesus fulfilled the Messianic prophecies of the Old Testament. It is because of these debates that Stephen was brought before the Sanhedrin and charged with blasphemy.

Saul was present when Stephen was dragged before the Sanhedrin. He listened as witnesses accused Stephen of preaching that the risen Christ would change the Law of Moses and destroy the Temple.

It's worth noting here what Jesus said shortly

before his Passion: *Destroy this temple and in three days I will raise it up.*[8] His enemies framed this as a threat, a diabolical taunt against the House of the Lord. In fact, it was *a prophecy of three distinct events: the destruction of the Temple, the Resurrection, and the establishment of a new Temple, the Church.* Rather than threaten to destroy the Temple, Jesus promised to raise it up—in fulfillment of the great Messianic prophecy to David, *your son shall build my Temple.*[9]

Stephen's response to the Sanhedrin takes up most of chapter 7 of Acts. Instead of responding directly to the charges against him, Stephen gives a summary of salvation history, extensively quoting and paraphrasing from many Old Testament books. He shows the depth of his learning and knowledge of the Scriptures. And he makes several key points.

First, Stephen defends himself masterfully with his retelling of biblical history. He demonstrates a consistent pattern of Israel rebelling against God's chosen ones and turns the table on his accusers: in their opposition to Jesus, *they* are the ones who are repeating it.

Stephen reminds his listeners of Joseph. Joseph saved the Israelites—at that time, consisting of just his brothers and their families—from starvation. *God was with him*, Stephen says; yet his brothers were jealous. They betray him and sell him into slavery. The pattern continues with Moses. As a young man, when still a member of Pharaoh's household, Moses tried to save and mediate for the Israelites. He too was rejected. *Who appointed you ruler and judge over us?*[10] one asks. It is the exact same question the chief priests and elders pose to Jesus: *By what authority are you doing these things?*[11]

Next, Stephen reminds the Sanhedrin of Moses' Messianic prophecy:

> God will raise up for you, from
> among your own kinsfolk, a
> prophet like me.*[12]*

God makes this promise to the Israelites after the terror of his theophany on Sinai, which sets even Moses trembling. It is a prophecy of Jesus, the one who speaks only what the Father commands,[13] and is also *like his brothers in every way.*[14]

Finally, regarding the Temple, Stephen points to God's theophany on Sinai and to his tabernacling for generations among the Israelites. The Temple has never been the exclusive dwelling place of God. God's words to Isaiah, which Stephen quotes, makes that abundantly clear:

> The heavens are my throne, the
>> earth is my footstool. What kind
>> of house can you build for me?[15]

As Stephen finishes his speech, he raises his eyes to heaven.

> Behold, I see the heavens opened
>> and the Son of Man standing at
>> the right hand of God.[16]

It is a vision of Jesus reigning in majesty. At his trial, Jesus had told Caiaphas and the Sanhedrin they would see him this way, as described in a Messianic prophecy of the prophet Daniel:

> I saw coming with the clouds of
>> heaven
> One like a son of man....
> He received dominion, splendor,
>> and kingship;
> all nations, peoples and tongues
>> will serve him.[17]

Stephen's discourse and vision of Jesus as Messiah inspire fury. His listeners drag him out of the city to stone him. Saul watches and approves as the rocks rain down. He hears the bones of his fellow Jew crack.

Right before he dies, Stephen utters eight simple words: *Lord, do not hold this sin against them.*[18] The words plant a seed that, in due time, will yield its harvest.

A Martyr's Prayer

The early Church writer Tertullian famously wrote that *the blood of the martyrs is the seed of the Church*. Tertullian saw this dynamic play out in the Roman persecutions. The principle is also at work in the very first days of the Church in the execution of the first martyr, Stephen.

Paul may have seemed unmoved at the trial and execution as he kept watch over the cloaks of those pummeling Stephen with their stones. Still, Stephen's courage and learning must have impressed him. And without doubt, Stephen's dying prayer of forgiveness helps obtain for Saul the grace of conversion. *The Church*, as St. Augustine noted, *owes Paul to the prayer of Stephen*.[19]

The seed that Stephen plants by his prayer and sacrifice does not sprout right away. Saul is committed to crushing the "followers of the Way." In Jerusalem, he goes from house to house arresting men and women and forcing others to flee.

Paul soon finds the Church has spread beyond Jerusalem. Diaspora Jews, such as the ones Peter preached to at Pentecost, have converted and returned home.

Saul pursues them in several foreign cities. Then he sets out for Damascus—and his encounter with the risen Christ.

Divine Mercy

Paul's encounter with Jesus is told or mentioned several times in the Bible—three times in *Acts*, twice in Paul's letters. It's a brief encounter, with incredible density. There's so much to unpack.

Paul's experience of Jesus is one *radiating* power. On the Cross and at his trial before Pilate, Jesus' power had been hidden, fulfilling Isaiah's prophecy: *He had no majestic bearing to catch our eye.*[20]

That's not the case here. Paul encounters Jesus as Messiah, clothed in majesty, ascended to the right hand of God. This is the risen Christ preached by Peter and the apostles, the Son of Man seen by Stephen before his death. His mere presence is enough to throw Paul and his detachment to their knees.

When Paul later writes to the Philippians from prison that *at the name of Jesus every knee should bend,*[21] he would have had this experience in mind. It is an experience of overwhelming power.

When Jesus appears to Paul, he calls him by name, twice:

> Saul, Saul, why are you persecuting me?

As he did with the apostles and so many during his public ministry, Jesus is communicating that he knows Paul,[22] that he has read his heart, and that he loves Paul, even though Paul is resisting him, *kicking against the goad.*[23]

Paul's absolute conviction that Christ knows and loves him personally is rooted in this moment and is expressed in his letters again and again.[24] *The Son of God*, Paul will write to the Galatians, *has loved me and given himself up for me*. To this day, we can still sense the note of marvel in his words.

Paul's encounter with Jesus on the road to Damascus is an encounter with Divine Mercy.

Jesus changes Paul in an instant from enraged inquisitor to the man who will author the greatest hymn to love ever penned:

> Love is patient; love is kind;

> It does not envy, it does not boast, it
> is not proud.
> It does not dishonor others,
> it is not self-seeking,
> it is not easily angered, it keeps no
> record of wrongs....
> Love never fails....
> Faith, hope, and love abide, these
> three;
> and the greatest of these is love.[25]

The love that pours from Jesus is not directed to Paul alone. Jesus expresses his deep bond with the Christians whom Paul is pursuing in the fascinating words of his rebuke: *Why are you persecuting me?*

This identification of the Lord with his disciples is something Paul has never experienced before. In the Old Testament, God calls his people his servants—*my servant Moses, my servant David, my servants the prophets.*[26]

Now, that servant relationship is gone. The followers of Jesus are no longer servants but friends,[27] members of his body, the Temple in which dwells the Spirit of God,[28] as Paul will write to the Corinthians.

As the Annunciation was for Mary, Jesus' appearance to Paul is a moment so rich he will ponder it the rest of his life. Though the encounter leaves him blind, he "sees" three things almost immediately.

First, Jesus is indeed the promised one of Israel, the Messiah.

Second, Stephen was correct: *The Most High does not dwell in houses made by human hands.*[29] The Church—the community of believers, the Body of Christ—is the living Temple of God.

And third, Jesus had chosen Paul to build up his Church with all the zeal, skill, and learning with which he had once attacked it.

Justification by Faith

Three days after his conversion, the Lord sent Ananias to pray over Paul, restore his sight, and baptize him. It took faith for Ananias to go; as a Christian leader in Damascus, Ananias was almost certainly one of those whom Paul had intended to bring back to Jerusalem in chains.

After his baptism, Paul goes to Arabia for three years. We know little of this time before the start of his ministry, or exactly where Paul went. "Arabia," for Paul, would have covered a vast area from the Red Sea to the Persian Gulf and included both the Sinai Peninsula and Jordan.

Paul gives the tantalizing detail in his Letter to

the Galatians that Mount Sinai—its precise location one of the great mysteries of the Bible—is in Arabia. Some have seen in this a hint that Paul spent his time in Arabia in retreat at the foot of Sinai, working out the implications and ramifications of *justification by faith*.

The apostles and the first disciples all have the experience before their great commission of re-reading the Scriptures in light of Christ's death, Resurrection, and Ascension and discovering its spiritual sense. We see two disciples undergo this experience in Luke's account of the Road to Emmaus. Paul's time in Arabia is his own "Road to Emmaus" period.

During his time studying under Gamaliel as his star pupil, Paul likely learned the Scriptures by heart. We can tell this by reading his letters, in which Paul effortlessly weaves together, paraphrases, and reinterprets Scripture passages from many different books of the Bible.

After his conversion, Paul reads Scripture afresh, now seeing its spiritual sense in all its richness. He reevaluates his understanding of the Mosaic ceremonial and religious law. He comes to see its provisional nature in God's plan—its status as a *paidagōgos,* or temporary guardian, as Paul calls it.[30]

The provisional nature of the Law was always

implicit in Scripture. After all, Abraham did not have the Law. As Paul will point out, Abraham was made righteous by an act of faith, of believing in God's promise of a descendant.[31] Throughout salvation history, from Abel through Noah, from Abraham through the patriarchs, from Moses through David, the good kings of Judah, and the prophets, it is *faith* that is the one common attribute of the heroes and heroines of Israel, not the practice (or flawless keeping) of the Law.

Once the Law was given at Sinai, of course, it was to be cherished and obeyed. The Israelites were to keep the Law zealously, allowing it to govern their actions and structure the external world.

Still, it was always acknowledged that only God could renew the spirit. Moses himself makes this clear at the end of the Book of Deuteronomy. He tells the Israelites that one day, after they have been scattered to the nations for disobedience, they will repent, and *The LORD, your God, will circumcise your hearts.*[32] When Paul later writes to the Romans that true circumcision is of the heart,[33] he is not refuting Moses; he is *citing* him.

Paul had treasured and meditated upon the word of God from his youth. As he ponders the Scriptures anew after his encounter with Christ, he finds what he had never seen before.

Practices such as circumcision, dietary and purity laws, and animal sacrifice could never give the full blessings God had promised his people. Their purpose was to anticipate and point to what would: Baptism, the life of grace, and the perfect sacrifice of God's own Son made present in the Eucharist.

The Mystical Body

With Christ's sacrifice, the ceremonial aspects of the Law had filled their purpose. God now asked for faith, faith in the one he had sent,[34] the Lord Jesus, and incorporation through baptism into his Mystical Body, the Church.

This had been God's plan from the very beginning. *For this reason a man shall leave his father and mother . . . and the two shall become one flesh.*[35] These words from the Book of Genesis are a beautiful description of marriage. But now Paul saw another meaning in them. The one-flesh union of husband and wife points to an even deeper union between Christ and his Church. From the beginning, God had intended men and women to be not just servants, not just friends, but members of his body —living stones of a Temple in which he would dwell, a Temple that would *fill the earth and subdue it.*[36]

The Messiah's kingdom had expanded; no longer limited to the circumcised, the ritually pure, the physical descendants of Abraham, the kingdom was now for all who, like Abraham, had faith—faith in his descendant, risen from the dead, in whom all the families of the world would be blessed. Its borders were no longer Israel's but the entire world, all creation in its great expanse through time and space.

It was this vision that would animate Paul when he returned from Arabia, fueling thirty years of missionary labors unequalled in the history of the Church.

Paul tells us in 1 Corinthians 15 that he has *toiled harder* than all the other apostles.[37] This is absolutely the case. After his conversion and time in Arabia, he spent three decades building the Church, visiting nearly fifty cities that we know of and establishing or strengthening local churches wherever he could.

Paul took at least three major missionary journeys, working his way around the Mediterranean basin from Damascus to Rome. He may even have travelled as far as Spain. During his travels, Paul was lashed five times in synagogues, beaten three times with rods, shipwrecked on three different occasions, bitten by a poisonous snake, and stoned.

Once Paul established a local church, he continued to care for and encourage it, writing letters, visiting, praying.[38] He does all this while supporting himself, at least in part, by tent making. And he participates in the first council of the Church, the Council of Jerusalem, in which he must argue strenuously that the Jewish law is not binding on Gentile converts.

The argument at the Council of Jerusalem on whether Gentile converts to Christianity are required to observe Jewish religious and ceremonial law is one in which the stakes could not be higher. Is the Messiah's kingdom simply for the Jewish people, the Israelites, or does it encompass the globe?

Paul, the preeminent Jewish scholar of his generation, has no doubt it is the latter. God had said through the prophet Isaiah that it is too small a thing for the Messiah simply to *restore the survivors of Israel*.[39] Till the end of his life, Paul will take to heart the rest of that verse, turning to it often to inspire him in his Herculean task:

> I have made you a light to the
>   Gentiles, that you may be an
>   instrument of salvation to the
>   ends of the earth.[40]

Paul's Christian life began with him bearing chains for others. It ended with him wearing them himself. Rather than silencing him, prison and chains provided another opportunity for evangelization.

When he was brought to Rome and placed under house arrest in AD 60, Paul continued to write to his churches and preach to visitors. He even witnessed to the praetorians who guarded him. *It has become clear throughout the whole palace guard and to everyone else that I am in chains for Christ,*[41] he would write to the Philippians. Paul's faith and courage impressed these elite soldiers, members of Caesar's household, and at least some embraced the faith. *My situation,* wrote Paul, *has turned out rather to advance the gospel.*

Chains did not prevent Paul from proclaiming the Gospel, and in the darkness of prison, his witness to Christ, Light of the Nations, shone all the brighter.

Paul's earthly mission would end a few years later when the executioner severed his head and won for him the martyr's crown. His work and witness would live on. The chains he bore so nobly for Christ would inspire countless others, in Caesar's household and beyond, to join him.

As we will see, two and a half centuries after Paul's imprisonment and martyrdom in Rome, the city and the empire itself would be won for the Messiah's kingdom, a prize and cherished possession placed underneath his feet.

8

TRIUMPH

ENEMIES UNDER YOUR FEET

Writing to the Romans near the middle of the first century, the Apostle Paul told his converts to respect civic rulers, including the emperor—*a servant of God for your good*.[1] In the autumn of AD 312, God's providence with respect to emperors was difficult to discern.

Diocletian had split the empire in AD 285. This led to instability; by the year 312, no fewer than four individuals claimed the supreme title *Augustus*. Diocletian and his co-emperors outlawed Christianity and viciously attacked the Church. It was the Great Persecution—perhaps the severest trial for God's people since Pharaoh's enslavement of the Israelites nearly two millennia earlier.

One of the *Augusti*, the emperor Constantine,

had, like his father before him, refused to participate, protecting Christians in Britannia and Gaul where he ruled. Now Constantine was headed to Rome to confront Maxentius, a tyrant who controlled Italy and Africa.

As Constantine and his soldiers marched, an emblem flashed on their shields. It was a Chi-Rho, the first two letters of the word *Christos*, or Christ. Constantine had adopted the Chi-Rho after Christ visited him in a dream—and after he and his entire army had seen a miraculous cross in the sky with words in Greek below it: *By this, conquer!*

As Constantine approached, Maxentius foolishly came out from behind Rome's walls to pursue him. When Constantine's soldiers charged, their Chi-Rhos blazing, Maxentius' forces panicked. Many, including Maxentius himself, drowned in the Tiber River attempting retreat.

The victory was a miracle. Constantine's triumphal arch, which stands in Rome to this day, affirms it. Observers could not help but compare Maxentius to Pharaoh,[2] who had also drowned with his army in foolish pursuit. Christians thanked God for their rescue, so similar to how God saved the Israelites long ago.

Yet there was a difference. Some sixteen centuries later, God had a face that could be portrayed, that one could look upon, and live. He had a name that could be written and proclaimed.

That name was Jesus, the *Christos*, the Messiah—the one whom Roman soldiers had mocked as "king of the Jews" and whose symbol now glinted on their triumphant shields.

CONSTANTINE'S VICTORY on October 28, 312 at the Battle of the Milvian Bridge was dramatic and sensational. The following year, Constantine and his co-emperor Licinius granted Christians legal status throughout the empire. Their Edict of Milan brought the Great Persecution to a close and allowed the Church, now comprising up to 10 percent of the empire, to assume its place in the public square.

Daniel's prophecy about the Messiah was becoming clear to see:

> He received dominion, splendor,
>   and kingship;
> all nations, peoples and tongues
>   will serve him.[3]

Fields Ripe for the Harvest

The Messiah's kingdom had begun at the Ascension; nine days later it had its first dramatic victory at Pentecost, with the baptism of three thousand people from many *nations, peoples, and tongues*. The Messiah's kingdom, the Church, had grown in the days and years that followed, one person, one soul at a time.

In its first generation the Church found, as the Lord Jesus had said, *fields ripe for the harvest*.[4] The Providence of God had shaped a world where the Gospel spread quickly, and where people were ready to receive it.

After receiving their Great Commission, the apostles and other missionaries traveled throughout the Mediterranean basin and beyond relatively quickly, benefitting both from Roman roads and the *Pax Romana* or Roman peace. In most places they could communicate in Greek. Greek was a common tongue or *lingua franca* over a vast area — a legacy of Alexander the Great.

Alexander bequeathed his subjects a language. The Jewish diaspora had given them something too; not a common religion, certainly, but a familiarity with beliefs and concepts such as monotheism, the holiness of God, and the dignity of those made in his image and likeness. Alexander had brought large swaths of the globe an appreciation of philosophy. The Jews had helped instill a sense of Providence. They introduced and bore witness to the idea that God had a plan for history and was active within it, leading his people *by testings, by signs and wonders, by war, by a mighty hand and outstretched arm, by great and awesome deeds.*[5]

At the time of Jesus the Jewish diaspora was present in almost every civilized city; the Greek author Strabo remarked that "it is not easy to find any place in the habitable world" where Jewish communities were not present and influential. [6] Diaspora Jews used the Greek Old Testament, the *Septuagint*, which was enormously influential. The Septuagint helped inspire Messianic expectations among the pagans, likely even influencing the great Roman poet Virgil. In a poem known as the *Fourth Eclogue*, written around 42 BC, Virgil writes of a coming Messianic age, in language very similar to Isaiah:

> Now the Virgin returns...a new
>   generation descends from
>   heaven on high...smile on the
>   birth of the child... He shall
>   have the gift of divine life...and
>   shall rule the world to which his
>   father's prowess brought

> peace.... The serpent too shall perish...See how all things rejoice in the age that is at hand![7]

The Church's first missionary efforts were through the network of diaspora Jewish synagogues. These communities had kept alive the promise of a Messiah. It was only natural to proclaim the good news of his arrival there first.

Diaspora synagogues were interesting places. They were houses of worship, though not the most solemn worship. Only in the Temple at Jerusalem were there animal sacrifices and burnt offerings. Only in the Temple was there a Holy of Holies, the inner sanctum that had once housed the Ark of the Covenant, to be entered only once a year, and only by the high priest.

Synagogues were places not of sacrifice but of prayer and reading the Scriptures. They were also community centers. Synagogues hosted lively discussions and debates on religious and philosophical topics, attended not only by the Jewish congregants and members but also often by non-Jews or Gentiles too. Most of these non-Jews were what is known as *metuentes* or God-fearers. They were Gentiles who were sympathetic to Judaism and adopted many Jewish beliefs and practices, without undergoing circumcision or observing all the ritual and dietary requirements of the Mosaic law. The centurion from Capernaum we read about in the Gospels is an example of a metuente or God-fearer. Though not Jewish himself, he was known to and admired by the Jewish leaders of Capernaum, for *he loves our nation and he built the synagogue for us.*[8] When the apostles and other first generation Christians, such as Stephen for example, went out and preached in the synagogues, they were addressing both Jews and Gentiles.[9]

Those who preached the Gospel encountered resistance. As we have seen with Stephen, arguments arose within the synagogues over whether Jesus was in fact the Messiah. Some who bore witness to Jesus were beaten or killed.

Even here, however, Divine Providence was at work. Expulsion from synagogues, what the apostle Paul called the *hardening of Israel,*[10] forced the first evangelists to proclaim the Gospel in the *streets and alleys*[11] of the world. Accusations led to public trials — and the opportunity to evangelize officials.

You will be led before governors and kings for my sake[12] Jesus had told the Apostles. And so it was.

The era of synagogue debates did not last long. The question about Jesus was a sword, separating Jews who proclaimed him Messiah from those who did not. The rupture accelerated in 70 AD, in the wake of one of the most cataclysmic events of history: The destruction of the second Temple.

A City Destroyed

Jesus predicted the destruction of the Jewish Temple, some forty years before it occurred. It is one of the most astounding prophecies ever made, and there is no question Jesus made it. Even his enemies acknowledged it, turning it into the false accusation that he had *threatened* the Temple[13] rather than foretelling its fate.

In 70 AD — within Christianity's first generation[14] — Jesus' prediction came to pass. The Temple was destroyed, not one stone left upon another.[15] It hasn't been rebuilt to this day.

In their siege of Jerusalem and destruction of the Second Temple, the Romans sent four legions against a relatively minor province. Rome wanted to crush the Judean revolt and make an example of the rebels for others. It was an unstable time for the empire. Several emperors had been killed or overthrown in quick succession, producing the "Year of the Four Emperors," in 69 AD. The year ended with Vespasian coming to power. Vespasian wanted to ensure a long reign and dynasty by quickly demonstrating his might and ruthlessness.

He did it in Judea, where his son Titus commanded the legions surrounding Jerusalem's walls.[16]

The historian Josephus tells us 1.1 million people died in the campaign against Jerusalem, overwhelmingly Jews. It is a staggering number for any era, nearly unfathomable for the ancient world. To this day, the siege and destruction of the Temple is remembered on the Jewish calendar with a day of mourning, *Tisha B'Av*.

The general, and later emperor, Titus celebrated his victory with an enormous parade through Rome. Titus displayed sacred artifacts plundered from the Temple, including the Menorah, as war trophies before the crowd.

Titus also built triumphal arches. One still stands near the Roman Forum. Another once marked the entrance to the Circus Maximus. Most of Rome's one million residents would pass under this arch each year, to take their seats in the Circus and watch chariot races, gladiatorial games — and the murder of Christians.

This arch is gone now, but its inscription is known from historical accounts:

> THE SENATE AND PEOPLE OF ROME DEDICATE THIS ARCH TO THE EMPEROR TITUS, WHO CONQUERED THE PEOPLE OF JUDEA AND

DESTROYED THE CITY OF JERUSALEM, WHICH ALL GENERALS, KINGS, AND PEOPLES BEFORE HIM FAILED TO DO OR EVEN ATTEMPT.[17]

It was the boast of a powerful oppressor of God's people, such as we have heard before: from Pharaoh to Moses; from Goliath to David; from Sennacherib to Hezekiah; from the Roman soldiers who taunted Jesus as they prepared to crucify him.

Jerusalem, the city of David, had from its earliest days exerted a mysterious fascination for kings. David's first act as king was conquering Jerusalem and making it his capital; the Persian king Cyrus is remembered to this day as an almost Messianic figure for his protection of Jerusalem, liberating it from the Babylonians and allowing the Jews to return there from exile.

The Queen of Sheba came to Jerusalem seeking wisdom. Alexander the Great visited Jerusalem too. When he arrived, he was astonished to recognize the vestments of the Jewish high priest; a similarly robed man had appeared to him in a dream, promising Alexander victory over the Persians. Alexander was convinced the God of the Jews was with him in battle. He honored the high priest, reverenced a tablet with the Divine Name, and offered sacrifice in the Temple.[18]

Throughout history, Jerusalem had been a beacon for good rulers who sought to serve their people. For the proud and arrogant, however, Jerusalem was a goad and a burr — a city whose walls, and above all its Temple, proclaimed that it is the Lord who is *king over all the earth*, who *rules over the nations*.[19] Pride, arrogance and defiance of God had driven the attacks of rulers such as Sennacherib, Nebuchadnezzar, and Antiochus IV. They reached their crescendo in the brutal campaign by Titus.

In destroying Jerusalem, Titus sought to exalt himself. His razing of the Temple was a taunt to all who hoped in God. It was a boast that Rome — not the Lord — ruled the nations. It was an assault on the assembly of God's people, an attempt to strike and scatter them with such ferocity they could never withstand Caesar again.

What Titus did not see is that in 70 AD the Temple was no longer the one place for the *ekklesia* or assembly of God's people. *My Father's house has many mansions*, Jesus said. In his kingdom, the place of encounter with God was wherever his apostles and priests spoke the words of institution and made present his Body and Blood. And with the coming of the Holy Spirit at Pentecost, the Temple of the Most High was no longer *a house made by human hands*, but the Church, his followers in whom his Spirit dwelled. In his campaign against Judea Titus destroyed a magnificent and sacred building. But the true Temple was now a mystical and spiritual reality that could *never* be destroyed.

Greeks Seek Wisdom

Titus' destruction of the Temple had enormous consequences for Jews and Christians alike. For Jews, it meant the rise of rabbinic Judaism, no longer centered on the Temple and sacrifice but on prayer and study. It meant a diminished status in the Empire, a loss of the gentile God-fearers they had once attracted.

For Christians, it accelerated the decline of Hebrew Christianity, practiced by the apostles and earliest believers, who worshipped as Christians while observing Jewish rites.

This was a loss, a real one. Hebrew Christians easily recognized Jesus as Messiah, the promised one of Israel, and so kept alive the knowledge and memory of how God had fulfilled his promises through the ages. But what was gained was a Christianity more open and attractive to the vast Gentile world...and an ever-greater fulfillment of the Church's role as a light to the nations.

After the destruction of the Jewish Temple,

many Gentiles who might once have explored Judaism sought out Christianity instead. Christianity also worshipped the God of Abraham, and had the monotheistic theology and moral code that had drawn the God-fearers. But it did so without requiring circumcision or kashrut. One could become a Christian through the painless and invisible mark of baptism. One could become a Christian and dine with pagan friends. Christianity made great demands, but it did not set its members visibly apart. That made it enormously attractive.

The classical world greatly admired the philosophers, who pursued wisdom at the expense of wealth, status, or worldly reward. There was a widely told tale in which Alexander the Great said if he must be someone other than himself, he'd most like to be Diogenes. Anyone who admired Diogenes and Socrates for their single-minded pursuit of virtue and wisdom would have to be intrigued by Jesus, who preached *Seek first the kingdom of God*.[20]

The Jewish people were uniquely set apart by God and prepared for the coming of the Messiah. Yet even in the pagan world there was an intuition of him. Some four hundred years before Christ, Plato asked readers of the *Republic* to contemplate, as the perfect exemplar of righteousness, *the just man who is thought unjust. This figure, says Plato, will be scourged, racked, bound...and at last, after suffering every kind of evil...impaled.*[21] For early Greek Christians... for Christians to this day...it seems a striking premonition of the Passion. It was a kind of pagan Greek version of the suffering servant passages of Isaiah, and helped prepare the Hellenistic world for Christ.

The Great Persecution

Whatever their role in society, Christians attracted. Christ, the Divine Logos, appealed to Greeks and others who esteemed wisdom. He who said *the last shall be first*[22] and called the heavy-burdened to come to him,[23] drew the poor and enslaved.

Christians, however, were sometimes resented. They poured out their lives, prayed for their enemies, loved each other. Yet when asked to render to others what belonged to God, they refused.

Woman vowed to chastity refused marriage. Soldiers refused to persecute; citizens and slaves refused sacrifice to the Emperor and pagan gods. It was above all the refusal to sacrifice that brought persecutions — the Great Persecution of Diocletian, and the ones that preceded it.

The early Christians were falsely accused of all

kinds of wickedness, but the most common charge was "atheism." In pagan Rome, atheism meant refusal to invoke or sacrifice to the pagan gods.

We might think Romans regarded their gods as legends or myths, but that's not true. For the Romans the gods were very real and powerful, capable of inflicting all kinds of punishments. By refusing to worship the gods, Romans believed Christians were angering them and thus putting the Empire at risk. St. Augustine wrote the *City of God* precisely to address this belief.[24]

Christians' refusal to worship the gods of Rome brought wave after wave of persecution over a nearly 250-year period...from Nero through Maximinus, Decius to Diocletian. Thousands were put to the cruelest tortures imaginable: torn with hooks; thrown to beasts; crucified; burned alive.

It's important to understand Christians believed in the reality of the pagan gods too. Primary sources such as St. Justin Martyr's *First Apology* are very clear about this.[25] The Roman gods were demons, demanding worship, as they had in every culture through the ages wherever they obtained a foothold. Their religious rites were designed to degrade their adherents, not only through idol worship but also through demands for licentiousness and ultimately human sacrifice. When Christians refused to participate these "gods" or demons went into a frenzy. They instigated the murders of thousands of men, women, and children in the most gruesome manner possible.

These were done as public spectacles in stadiums such as the Circus Maximus, so crowds could be corrupted by cheering and laughing at their torments.

The persecutions were diabolical. The Apostle Paul, himself a one-time persecutor, had warned Christians they struggled not only with flesh and blood, but with *powers and principalities*, and *evil spirits in the heaven*.[26] Nowhere was that struggle more stark than in Rome's Circus Maximus... where crowds entered under a Triumphal Arch boasting of Titus' destruction of Jerusalem...then cheered as Christians were *damnatio ad bestias* — condemned to the beasts — or killed in other grisly ways.

The early Christian martyrs refused to worship demons. They chose the path of the Lord Jesus, who during his temptation in the desert had rebuffed Satan's demand for worship. They chose the way of the Cross.

And as the Cross for Jesus led to his rising and enthronement as Messiah, so too did the martyrs' sufferings lead to triumph. The spectacle of their martyrdoms, meant to terrorize the Church into submission, instead revolted the crowds at what their Empire had become. The very blackness of what the West had descended into revealed all the more the beauty of the Holy Spirit, animating those who gave their lives for Christ.

> And though the last lights off the
>   black West went
> Oh, morning, at the brown brink
>   eastward, springs —
> Because the Holy Ghost over
>   the bent
> World broods with warm breast and
>   with ah! bright wings.[27]

You Have Conquered, O Galilean

The Empire's wave of persecutions against the Church grew progressively more severe, reaching a fever pitch under Diocletian. With every persecution, the number of Christians grew. The sheer inhumanity of the treatment of Christians forced the Romans to confront whether they wanted to be in thrall to the gods who demanded it. And the Romans had to ask themselves, who really represented the best of Rome? As the early Church writer Tertullian pointed out, Romans had a long history of admiring those who faced death bravely in fidelity to some high or noble cause.[28] No Roman hero faced death more bravely than the Christians. Girls and children went to terrible deaths with more courage than Hector heading out to face the wrath of Achilles.

Persecution did not kill the Church. It made it stronger. In holding fast to Christ in the trials of the arena, the martyrs vanquished the gods.

The trials of the martyrs ended with Constantine's victory at the Battle of the Milvian Bridge. Paganism made one last attempt to rear its head. In 360 AD Julius was named Augustus. Julius had been baptized and raised Christian, but had rejected the faith. He attempted to suppress it through various measures, including an unexpected one: Ordering the rebuilding of the Temple in Jerusalem.

The ancients were now acutely aware that Christ had predicted the destruction of the Temple. Julian wanted to prove Christ wrong by rebuilding it. He knew as well the destruction of the Temple had helped spread Christianity throughout the empire. Perhaps Julian believed that while the worship of the one God, the Lord, could not be suppressed, it could be contained as it had been in the past, centered on and limited to one sacred site.

The amazing thing is Julian could not rebuild

the Temple. A severe earthquake struck Jerusalem in 363. There were other hazards as well. A contemporary and admirer of Julian's, the historian Ammianus Marcellinus, records that fearful balls of fire inexplicably appeared repeatedly at the building site, killing workmen and forcing them to call off the effort.[29] To this day it has never been completed.

That same year Julian fell to an enemy spear while on campaign in Persia. His dying words, perhaps apocryphal, were the words of dying pagan Rome to the one who would replace it.

You have conquered O Galilean.

THE WORDS of Julian the Apostate, *You have conquered, O Galilean*, answered the question posed by his fellow citizen Pontius Pilate to Jesus of Nazareth some 330 years earlier: *Are you the king of the Jews?*

Yes.

By 363 AD, even the apostate emperor Julian was forced to acknowledge: Jesus was indeed king of the Jews.

He was the Messiah, more powerful than the Emperor. The Messiah's kingdom was the most dominant force within the Empire. And it was present well beyond it, with outposts in Armenia, India, Ethiopia, and more.

Through his mystical body, the Church, Jesus had gathered the lost sheep of Israel. His apostles had preached the Gospel, not only in Jerusalem and Judea, but in the synagogues of the vast Jewish diaspora, in Antioch and Alexandria, Asia and Rome. There they had encountered, not only Jews, but God-fearing Gentiles. These Gentiles were now invited into covenant with him, without the need for circumcision, or special diets, or other burdens of the Law.

For both Jew and Gentile, the new covenant was entered through baptism and faith in Christ — a faith prefigured by Abraham, and Moses, and David, and the great heroes of God's people of long ago.

As Jesus had predicted, the Jewish Temple was no more, torn to the ground by the Romans, with not one stone remaining. But the loss of the Temple had not extinguished the presence of the Lord. His Real Presence had been brought to thousands of cities and towns and communities. An acceptable and everlasting sacrifice was made daily in churches throughout the world, in the Holy Mass.

Three hundred and thirty years after his crucifixion, it was apparent to even the jaundiced eye of the apostate emperor Julian that Jesus had fulfilled the Messianic promises. The Son of David had established his kingdom, and raised a new Temple, the Church. He had gathered the tribes of Israel. He had been a light to the nations. And he had put his enemies under his feet.

There was then, as now, more people to be invited into his kingdom, his covenant. There were more great saints and apostles to be made; more lands and peoples and works to be consecrated to him, to be placed under his glorious rule. This would be the task, the only true task and purpose, of history. And it would continue, and will continue, until he comes again, as Messiah, to judge the world, and place the last enemy, death, under his feet.

END

NOTES

1. Exodus

1. Jn 8:58.
2. Mt 27:11; Mk 15:2; Lk 23:3; Jn 18:33.
3. Mk 14:61.
4. Scholars propose a range of dates for the Exodus, most falling between 1200 and 1500 BC.
5. Gn 37.
6. Gn 50:20.
7. Gn 48:5.
8. Gn 49:10.
9. Ex 1:8.
10. James Henry Breasted, *A History of the Ancient Egyptians* (London: Smith, Elder & Company, 1908), p. 252.
11. Ex 2:11–14.
12. Ex 5:2.
13. Mt 7:2.
14. Ex 12:12; Nm 33:4.
15. Dt 32:17; 1 Cor 10:20.
16. St. Justin Martyr, *The First Apology*, chap 5.
17. Ex 8:19.
18. Ex 12:12.
19. Ex 15:1–18.
20. Dt 18:15–18.
21. Ex 31:18.
22. Ex 19:6.
23. Rom 2:15.
24. Is 55:8.
25. Ex 16:3.
26. Jn 10:11.
27. Ps 78:52.

28. Jn 14:18.
29. Mt 6:11; Lk 11:3.
30. Ex 16:20.
31. Nm 14:6–9.
32. Nm 14:22–23.
33. Nm 20:8–12.
34. Ps 99:1–3 NABRE.

2. David

1. Dt 17:14–20.
2. 1 Sm 13:14; Acts 13:22.
3. 1 Sm 9:2.
4. 1 Sm 9:21.
5. 1 Sm 13.
6. 1 Sm 16.
7. 2 Sm 11.
8. Ex 30:11–16; 1 Chr 21; 2 Sm 24.
9. Jn 8:29.
10. 1 Sm 18:7.
11. 1 Sm 18:11.
12. Jn 1:15.
13. 1 Sm 24:4; 1 Sm 26:12.
14. Mt 5:44.
15. 2 Sm 5:4.
16. Lk 3:23.
17. 2 Sm 5:6.
18. Jn 5:1–18.
19. Heb 7:3.
20. Ps 110:4.
21. Gn 22:8.
22. Gn 22:14.
23. John J. Parsons, "Jacob's Dream of Messiah," *Hebrew4Christians*, March 13, 2019, www.hebrew4christians.com/Scripture/Parashah/Summaries/Vayetzei/Ladder/ladder.html.
24. 2 Sm 24:25.

25. 2 Sm 7:12–14 NABRE.
26. 2 Sm 7:16.
27. Ps 110:1, 2 NABRE.
28. Mt 22:44.
29. 1 Kgs 10:24.
30. Is 49:6.
31. In addition to David, the Worthies are Hector, Alexander the Great, Julius Caesar, Joshua, Judas Maccabeus, King Arthur, Charlemagne, and the crusader Godfrey of Bouillon.
32. Ben Jonson, *To the Memory of My Beloved the Author, Mr. William Shakespeare.*
33. Jeffrey Kranz, "Which Old Testament Book did Jesus Quote Most?" *Biblia Blog*, April 30, 2014, http://blog.biblia.com/2014/04/which-old-testament-book-did-jesus-quote-most/.
34. Ps 23:1–4.
35. Mt 28:20.

3. Exile

1. 2 Kgs 25.
2. 1 Kgs 12:14 NABRE.
3. Ex 19:6.
4. 1 Kgs 11:30–39.
5. Dt 12:5–6.
6. 2 Kgs 17:17.
7. Eric Niderost, "Jerusalem: Surviving the Second Siege by Assyrian King Sennacherib," *Warfare History Network*, October 3, 2018, www.warfarehistorynetwork.com/daily/military-history/jerusalem-surviving-the-second-siege-by-assyrian-king-sennacherib/.
8. 2 Kgs 18:33, 35 NABRE.
9. Gn 49:10.
10. According to 2 Mc 2, the Ark was hidden in a cave on Mount Nebo by the prophet Jeremiah. It is to remain there undiscovered *until God gathers his people together again and shows them mercy* (2 Mc 2:7).

11. Jer 22:30.
12. Is 52:3, 1 Pt 1:18–19.
13. Gn 22:8.
14. Jer 23:3 NABRE.
15. Jer 23:5 NABRE.
16. Jer 33:18.
17. Hos 3:5.
18. Zec 10:8–10; 12:8.
19. Ez 37:21–28.
20. Is 11:10–12.
21. Ez 37:27 NABRE.
22. 1 Kgs 11:39.
23. Ez 37:24 NABRE.
24. Is 49:5.
25. Is 49:3.
26. Is 49:6 NABRE.
27. Is 42:3 NABRE.
28. Zec 9:9; Mt 21:4–5; Jn 12:14–16.
29. Is 42:1, 6, 7 NABRE.
30. 1 Sm 8:17.

4. Trial

1. Jn 1:41.
2. Mt 16:16–18.
3. Mt 14:3–12; Mk 6:17–29.
4. Mt 11:3; Lk 7:19.
5. Rom 1:3.
6. Mi 5:1 NABRE.
7. Jn 1:46.
8. Jer 22:24–30. For a discussion of the curse of Jeconiah and how it relates to the Messiah, see Arnold Fruchtenbaum, "The Genealogy of the Messiah," *Jews for Jesus*, https://m.jewsforjesus.org/publications/issues/issues-v05-n06/the-genealogy-of-the-messiah/.
9. Mt 12:24; Mk 3:22; Lk 11:15. See also Glenn Miller, "Were the Miracles of Jesus invented by the Disciples/Evangelists?"

Christian Thinktank, June 19, 2002, http://christianthinktank.com/mq12.html for an excellent overview of extra biblical early references to the miracles of Jesus.
10. See *Catechism of the Catholic Church* (CCC), no. 1286.
11. Dt 17:15.
12. Mt 1:18.
13. Mt 11:9–11.
14. Lk 1:15.
15. Jn 3:34.
16. Lk 3:22.
17. 2 Sm 7:14.
18. Is 42:1.
19. Mt 19:28.
20. Jn 18:36.
21. Mt 7:28–29; Mk 1:22; Lk 4:32.
22. Jn 10:11–16.
23. Jn 2:13–17.
24. Ex 30:11–16.
25. Rv 21:27.
26. Mt 10:30; Lk 12:7.
27. Is 42:7.
28. Lk 5:20–22.
29. Jn 2:1–11.
30. Mt 14:15–21; Mk 6:34–44; Lk 9:12–17; Jn 6:1–13.
31. Mt 9:18–26; Mk 5:21–43; Lk 8:40–56.
32. Lk 7:11–17.
33. Jn 11:1–44.
34. Gn 2:5.
35. Lk 11:20; Ex 8:15.
36. Mt 22:41–46; Mk 12:35–37; Lk 20:41–44.
37. A few examples: Jn 1:45–49; Jn 4:29; Mk 10:21.
38. E. E. Cummings, *"my father moved through dooms of love."*
39. Is 42:3; Mt 12:20.
40. Lk 4:18–19 NABRE; Is 61:1–2.
41. 1 Sm 8:17.
42. Mt 20:25–27 NABRE; see also Mk 10:42–45; Lk 22:25–26.
43. Mt 15:21–28; Mk 7:24–30.
44. Mt 8:5–13; Lk 7:1–10.

5. Ascension

1. Mt 27:46.
2. 1 Cor 15:6.
3. Acts 2:34–35; 1 Pt 3:22.
4. 1 Cor 15:25.
5. Mt 22:44.
6. Ex 17:1–7; 1 Cor 10:4.
7. Jn 19:34.
8. Mt 26:53.
9. Jn 19:10–11.
10. Mt 26:39; Mk 14:36; Lk 22:42.
11. Gn 3:15.
12. Gn 3:15.
13. Jn 12:31.
14. The account of the temptation of Jesus is told in Mt 4:1–11 and Lk 4:1–13. The order of temptations here follows Luke rather than Matthew, with Luke portraying the satanic entry into Jerusalem and proposed mockery of sacrifice as the climactic conclusion to the temptation account.
15. Phil 2:6–8.
16. Col 1:13.
17. 1 Pt 1:18–19.
18. Lk 24.
19. Heb 11:19.
20. 1 Chr 21:18–27; 2 Sm 24:18–25.
21. Gn 22:8.
22. Acts 2:31.
23. Acts 2:25–27 NABRE; Ps 16:8–10.
24. Mt 27:46.
25. Ps 22:7–9 NABRE.
26. Ps 22:17–18 NABRE.
27. Is 53:3.
28. Is 50:6 NABRE.
29. St. Jerome, *Prologue to Isaiah*.
30. Is 53:5.
31. Lk 1:26–38.

32. Is 7:14.
33. 2 Sm 7:14.
34. Jer 22:30.
35. Lk 2:22–35.
36. Lk 2:51.
37. Jn 1:29.
38. Mt 26:12; Mk 14:8; Jn 12:7.
39. Dt 17:15.
40. Acts 10:38.
41. See CCC 664.

6. Pentecost

1. Acts 2:15.
2. Ex 19:18; Acts 2:3.
3. CCC 703.
4. Gn 1:2.
5. 1 Sm 16:13.
6. Jn 3:34.
7. Jn 16:7.
8. See CCC 1287.
9. Peter J. Vaghi, "*The Upper Room in Jerusalem: The Most Important Room in Christendom*," Franciscan Media, blog, https://www.franciscanmedia.org/the-upper-room-in-jerusalem-the-most-important-room-in-christendom/.
10. St. Epiphanius of Salamis, *Weights and Measures*, section 14.
11. Lk 22:19; 1 Cor 11:23–24.
12. Jn 13:1–17.
13. Jn 14–17.
14. Jn 15:15.
15. Jn 20.
16. Jn 3:1–2; 19:38.
17. Mark's mother is the owner of the Christian house church referenced in Acts 12:12; some identify this home with the Upper Room.
18. Lk 22:10–12.
19. Mt 10:32.

20. See David Christian Clausen, *The Upper Room and Tomb of David: The History, Art and Archaeology of the Cenacle on Mount Zion* (Jefferson, NC: McFarland, 2016) for the most comprehensive examination of this question. An overview of Clausen's findings is given by Marek Dospěl, "Did Jesus' Last Supper Take Place Above the Tomb of David?" *Bible History Daily*, March 29, 2018, www.biblicalarchaeology.org/daily/biblical-sites-places/jerusalem/jesus-last-supper-tomb-of-david/ww.example.com.
21. Acts 2:29.
22. Ps 2:6.
23. Mt 7:6.
24. Josephus, *Antiquities of the Jews*, 16:7.
25. Lk 2:25–32.
26. Jn 8:56.
27. Mt 17:1–8; Mk 9:2–8; Lk 9:28–36.
28. 2 Sm 7:12–14.
29. Is 11:1–2.
30. Jer 23:3.
31. For estimates of the historical Jewish population in Judea and the diaspora, see Joseph Jacobs, "Statistics," Jewish Encyclopedia (New York: Funk and Wagnalls, 1906), www.jewishencyclopedia.com/articles/13992-statistics. See also *Encyclopaedia Brittanica Online*, Louis H. Feldman, et al., s.v. "Judaism: Religion," last updated February 8, 2019, www.britannica.com/topic/Judaism.
32. Ps 84:2–4 NABRE.
33. Zec 12:10.
34. Acts 2:36–38.
35. 1 Cor 1:23.
36. Acts 2:23.
37. Gn 50:20.
38. 1 Cor 15:6.
39. Ez 37.
40. Jas 1:1.
41. Jn 4:20–24.
42. Jn 2:19.
43. Jn 14:2.

44. Mt 18:20.
45. Ez 37:26.
46. Jer 33:18.
47. Gerard Manley Hopkins, SJ, *As kingfishers catch fire*.
48. Acts 21:20. Though most translations reference "thousands of Jews," the Greek word *myriad* means literally tens of thousands.
49. C. Park, "Religion and geography," in J. Hinnells, ed., *Routledge Companion to the Study of Religion* (London: Routledge, 2004).

7. Paul

1. Acts 9:4–6.
2. Acts 22:28.
3. Gal 1:14.
4. Phil 3:5–6.
5. Rom 11:1; Phil 3:5.
6. Cf. Ps 1:1–3.
7. 2 Chr 7:19–20.
8. Mt 26:61; 27:40; Jn 2:19.
9. 2 Sm 7:13.
10. Ex 2:14.
11. Mt 21:23; Mk 11:28; Lk 20:2.
12. Acts 7:37; Dt 18:15.
13. Jn 12:49.
14. Heb 2:17.
15. Acts 7:49; Is 66:1.
16. Acts 7:56; cf. Ps 110:1.
17. Dn 7:13–14.
18. Acts 7:60.
19. Cf. St. Augustine, *Sermons on the New Testament*, Sermon 6, Section 3.
20. Is 53:2.
21. Phil 2:10.
22. Cf. 1 Cor 13:12.
23. Acts 26:14.

24. Gal 1:15–16; 2:20; 1 Cor 13:12.
25. 1 Cor 13.
26. For example: Nm 12:7; Jo 1:2; Ps 89:20; Am 3:7.
27. Jn 15:15
28. 1 Cor 3:16.
29. Acts 7:48.
30. Gal 3:23–25.
31. Gn 15:6; Rom 4:3.
32. Dt 30:6.
33. Rom 2:29.
34. Jn 6:29.
35. Gn 2:24; Eph 5:31.
36. Gn 1:28.
37. 1 Cor 15:10.
38. 2 Cor 11:24–28.
39. Is 49:6.
40. Acts 13:47.
41. Phil 1:13.

8. Triumph

1. Rom 13:4.
2. Cf. Eusebius, *Life of Constantine*, Chapter 38, "Death of Maxentius on the Bridge of the Tiber."
3. Dn 7:13–14.
4. Jn 4:35; cf also Lk 10:2; Mt 9:37;
5. Dt 4:34
6. As quoted by Josephus (*Antiquities* XIV, 7.2)
7. Excerpt from Virgil's Fourth Eclogue. Compare with Is 7:14, 9:1-6, 11:6-8
8. cf Lk 7:5
9. cf Acts 13:16
10. Rom 11:25
11. Lk 14:21
12. Mt 10:18
13. Mt 26:61; Acts 6:14
14. Mt 24:34

15. Mt 24:2
16. Gurevich, David *Why Did Vespasian and Titus Destroy Jerusalem?*, TheTorah.com
17. Taken from http://www.thehistoryblog.com/archives/36814 the Codex Einsidlensis (Eisniedeln mss 326) which records the inscription in Inscriptiones Urbis Romae)
18. Josephus, *Jewish antiquities* 11.325-336
19. Ps 47:9-10
20. Mt 6:33
21. Plato, *The Republic*, Book II
22. Mk 10:31; Mt 19:30; Lk 13:30
23. Mt 11:28
24. St. Augustine, *The City of God*. From the Preface: *The glorious city of God is my theme in this work...I have undertaken its defense against those who prefer their own gods to the Founder of this city...*
25. St. Justin Martyr, *The First Apology*, chap 5
26. Eph 6:12
27. Gerard Manley Hopins, SJ, *God's Grandeur* (excerpt)
28. Tertullian, *Apology*, chap 50
29. Marcellinus, Ammianus. *Roman Antiquities*, Book 23 Section 1.3.

ABOUT THE AUTHOR

Rick Rotondi is the writer and executive producer of *Messiah* and the founder of Cenacle. A publishing veteran, Rotondi is the co-writer of *Queen of Heaven* and the author of *101 Surprising Facts About the Bible*.

ABOUT MESSIAH

This book is adapted from the Cenacle film series *Messiah* — an exploration of the messianic prophecies of the Bible, and how they were fulfilled by Jesus, both during his earthly life, and after.

Hosted by Leonardo Defilippis and filmed at nearly 30 locations in the United States, the Holy Land, and Rome, *Messiah*'s eight episodes feature live-action narration supplemented with expert commentary, dramatic voice acting, hundreds of classic artworks, and nearly two dozen songs, orchestral performances and hymns. Learn more at SeeMessiah.com

www.ingramcontent.com/pod-product-compliance
Lightning Source LLC
Chambersburg PA
CBHW030111100526
44591CB00009B/368